Practical social work

Published in conjunction with
the British Association of Social Workers

THE BRITISH ASSOCIATION OF SOCIAL WORKERS

Social work is at an important stage in its development. The profession is
facing fresh challenges to work flexibly in fast-changing social and
organisational environments. New requirements for training are also
demanding a more critical and reflective, as well as more highly skilled,
approach to practice.

The British Association of Social Workers (www.basw.co.uk) has always
been conscious of its role in setting guidelines for practice and in seeking
to raise professional standards. The concept of the *Practical Social Work*
series was conceived to fulfil a genuine professional need for a carefully
planned, coherent series of texts that would stimulate and inform
debate, thereby contributing to the development of practitioners' skills
and professionalism.

Newly relaunched, the series continues to address the needs of all those
who are looking to deepen and refresh their understanding and skills. It is
designed for students and busy professionals alike. Each book marries
practice issues and challenges with the latest theory and research in a
compact and applied format. The authors represent a wide variety of
experience both as educators and practitioners. Taken together, the books
set a standard in their clarity, relevance and rigour.

A list of new and best-selling titles in this series follows overleaf.
A comprehensive list of titles available in the series, and further details
about individual books, can be found online at:
www.palgrave.com/socialworkpolicy/basw

Series standing order ISBN 978–0–333–80313–4

You can receive future titles in this series as they are published by placing a standing order. Please contact your bookseller or, in the case of
difficulty, contact us at the address below with your name and address,
the title of the series and the ISBN~~~~~~~~

Cust..ion Ltd, Houndmills,
Basi

D1141739

Practical social work series
Founding Editor: Jo Campling

New and best-selling titles

Robert Adams *Empowerment, Participation and Social Work* (4th edition)
Sarah Banks *Ethics and Values in Social Work* (4th edition)
James G. Barber *Social Work with Addictions* (2nd edition)
Christine Bigby and Patsie Frawley *Social Work Practice and Intellectual Disability*
Suzy Braye and Michael Preston-Shoot *Practising Social Work Law* (3rd edition)
Veronica Coulshed and Audrey Mullender with David N. Jones and Neil Thompson
    Management in Social work (3rd edition)
Veronica Coulshed and Joan Orme *Social Work Practice* (5th edition)
Lena Dominelli *Anti-Racist Social Work* (3rd edition)
Celia Doyle *Working with Abused Children* (4th edition)
Richard Ingram, Jane Fenton, Ann Hodson and Divya Jindal-Snape *Reflective Social Work
    Practice*
Gordon Jack and Helen Donnell *Social Work with Children*
Tony Jeffs and Mark K. Smith (editors) *Youth Work Practice*
Joyce Lishman *Communication in Social Work* (2nd edition)
Paula Nicolson and Rowan Bayne: *Psychology for Social Work Theory and Practice*
    (4th Edition)
Michael Oliver,Bob Sapey and Pam Thomas *Social Work with Disabled People*
    (4th edition)
Joan Orme and David Shemmings *Developing Research Based Social Work Practice*
Terence O'Sullivan *Decision Making in Social Work* (2nd edition)
Mo Ray and Judith Phillips *Social Work with Older People* (5th edition)
Michael Preston-Shoot *Effective Groupwork* (2nd edition)
Jerry Tew *Working with Mental Distress*
Neil Thompson *Anti-Discriminatory Practice* (5th edition)
Alan Twelvetrees *Community Work* (4th edition)

Richard Ingram,
Jane Fenton,
Ann Hodson
and
Divya Jindal-Snape

Reflective Social Work Practice

palgrave
macmillan

THE BRITISH ASSOCIATION OF SOCIAL WORKERS

First published 2014 by
PALGRAVE MACMILLAN

Palgrave Macmillan in the UK is an imprint of Macmillan Publishers Limited, registered in England, company number 785998, of Houndmills, Basingstoke, Hampshire RG21 6XS.

Palgrave Macmillan in the US is a division of St Martin's Press LLC, 175 Fifth Avenue, New York, NY 10010.

Palgrave Macmillan is the global academic imprint of the above companies and has companies and representatives throughout the world.

Palgrave® and Macmillan® are registered trademarks in the United States, the United Kingdom, Europe and other countries

ISBN: 978–1–137–30198–7

This book is printed on paper suitable for recycling and made from fully managed and sustained forest sources. Logging, pulping and manufacturing processes are expected to conform to the environmental regulations of the country of origin.

A catalogue record for this book is available from the British Library.

A catalog record for this book is available from the Library of Congress.

Typeset by Cambrian Typesetters, Camberley, Surrey

Printed in China

Brief contents

List of illustrations *x*

Acknowledgements *xii*

1 Introduction: the social work context *1*

2 Dynamics of critical reflection and reflexivity *17*

3 Communications skills for building and sustaining relationships *35*

4 Undertaking life-changing assessments *50*

5 Critically informed interventions *68*

6 Making significant risk decisions *85*

7 Meetings *101*

8 Records and report writing *117*

9 Effective supervision – reflection, support and direction *130*

10 From a reflective social work practitioner to a reflective social work organization *148*

References *159*

Index *171*

Contents

List of illustrations *x*

Acknowledgements *xii*

1 Introduction: the social work context *1*
Practitioner's context *2*
Policy direction into action *5*
Key themes *8*
The Reflective Social Work Practitioner Model *13*
How to use this book *14*
A guide to the chapters *15*

2 Dynamics of critical reflection and reflexivity *17*
Critical reflection *17*
Reflexivity *29*
Conclusion *33*

3 Communication skills for building and sustaining relationships *35*
Communication and reflection: a starting point *37*
A framework for reflecting about communication *40*
Communication and working with resistance *44*
Conclusion *48*

4 Undertaking life-changing assessments *50*
Assessment and influencing factors *53*
Understanding the role of reflection in
    assessment *57*

Emotions and assessment 58

Power, empowerment and the value base of
assessment 60

Analysing and completing an assessment 63

Conclusion 65

5 Critically informed interventions 68

Linking and differentiating assessment and
intervention 71

Identifying the beginning and end of intervention:
the influence of hard and soft features 75

Intervention and anti-oppressive practice 79

Applying the reflective practitioner models to
intervention 81

Conclusion 83

6 Making significant risk decisions 85

Defensible risk decisions 88

Engaging with risk and need 92

Critical reflection 93

Risks and rights 94

Subjective factors affecting risk assessment 97

Conclusion 100

7 Meetings 101

The meeting: a particular context 104

Group dynamics and knowledge 105

Power dynamics 108

Strategies in meetings 111

Conclusion 113

8 Records and report writing 117

The place of writing in social work 119

Reflection and writing 122

Writing, professionalism and relationships 124

Conclusion 127

9 **Effective supervision: reflection, support and direction** *130*

The role of supervision *133*
A collaborative approach to reflective supervision *136*
Out-sourced modes of supervision *140*
Informal support network and reflection *141*
Organizational culture and reflection *144*
Conclusion *146*

10 **From a reflective social work practitioner to a reflective social work organization** *148*
Features of reflective social work practice *149*
Professionalism *150*
Relationship-based work *152*
Reflective organizations *153*
Conclusion *155*

References *159*

Index *171*

List of illustrations

Figures

Figure 1.1: The Reflective Social Work Practitioner Model *14*
Figure 2.1: Single-loop rational-technical practice *18*
Figure 2.2: Double-loop critically reflective practice *19*
Figure 9.1: Supervision: focus on outcomes and critical reflection *137*
Figure 9.2: An example of a mismatch in expectations between supervisor and supervisee *138*
Figure 10.1 The Reflective Social Work Organization Model *156*

Tables

Table 2.1: Analysis of Models of Reflection *22*
Table 10.1: Grid to evaluate 'How reflective is my organization?' *157*

Boxes

Box 2.1: Example of single-loop reflection *18*
Box 2.2: Example of double-loop reflection *20*
Box 2.3: Questions to prompt reflection and reflexivity *30*
Box 2.4: Examples of questions to deepen critical reflection to move towards reflexivity *31*

Box 3.1: A framework for reflection on
   communication in social work *41*

Diaries

Aileen's diary (Education Social Worker) *35*
Steve's diary (Hospital Social Worker) *50*
Tracy's Diary (Adult, Community-Based Team Social
   Worker) *68*
Erika's Diary (Criminal Justice Worker) *85*
Susan's Diary (Care Manager) *101*
Rashid's Diary (Manager of Young Person's
   Residential Unit, Key Worker for Robbie) *117*
Sandra's diary (Social worker based in a local
   authority, dealing with young offenders) *130*

Acknowledgements

We wish to acknowledge our sincere gratitude to our colleague Regan Shaw for insightful discussions about critical reflection and the analysis of models of reflection. We are also indebted to our other colleagues and service users with whom we have worked over the years. Without our dialogues and experiences with them, this book would not have been possible.

We would also like to thank Lloyd Langman and Helen Caunce of Palgrave Macmillan for their continuous guidance and encouragement, from the conception to the completion of this book. We are also grateful to India Annette-Woodgate and Alec McAulay for their excellent and patient support.

Finally, we would like to express our love and thanks to our families for their never ending support and patience.

The authors and publisher would like to thank the following publishers and organisations for permission to reproduce copyright material:

Ashgate Publishing and Bairbre Redmond for their permission to reproduce the 'Double-loops critically reflective practice' model and the 'Single-loop rational-technical practice' model from B. Redmond (2006) *Reflection in Action: Developing reflective practice in health and social services* (adapted with the permission of Ashgate Publishing and Bairbre Redmonds), p. 45.

Journal of Applied Academic Practice for permission to reproduce the 'Supervision: focus on outcomes and critical reflection' model and the 'An example of a mismatch in expectations between supervisor and supervisee' model from D. Jindal-Snape and R. Ingram (2013) 'Understanding and Supporting Triple Transitions of International Doctoral Students: ELT and SuReCom Models', *Journal of Perspectives in Applied Academic Practice*, 1(1), pp. 17–24.

CHAPTER 1

Introduction: the social work context

Welcome to *Reflective Social Work Practice*. This book is designed to locate the process of reflection within the ordinary, day-to-day practice of front-line social workers.

As will be seen, chapters are organized around the kinds of activities social workers undertake. Diary extracts deliberately establish the book as a practical resource, relevant to any practitioner or student social worker undertaking any of the social work activities. As a result, the book an essential companion for social workers, enabling them to make practical links between the use of reflection and their own practice experiences regardless of context. The emphasis on the 'week in the life' of a social worker allows the role of reflection to be embedded in the broad range of activities and roles that a social worker may be involved at points within their working week. The additional worth of the book, however, lies in the deconstruction of those activities in terms of reflective and reflexive practice, and in the purposeful attention to the integration of values, emotions and relationship-building within that process. It is very timely as the role of reflection in social work practice now occupies a central place in professional frameworks and narratives. For example, the Professional Capabilities Framework (PCF) (College of Social Work, 2012) highlights critical reflection as one of its nine domains. There is an emphasis on the importance of critical thinking in the complex world of social work practice and the necessity of it being evident at student, practitioner and management levels. Simply put, reflective practice is at the heart of practice throughout the entirety of a social worker's career regardless of context or role.

This chapter will also:

- illustrate the current context of social work practice
- consider how policy is translated into actual practice
- highlight the key themes of the book
- introduce the 'Reflective Social Work Practitioner Model'
- orientate the reader to the content of later chapters.

Practitioner's context

Social work practice in any setting is contextualized by a number of key, 'hard' features such as legislation, policy, procedure and theory. These elements are defined as 'hard' features because they are transparently evident, relatively easily articulated in their application, essential, and part of any robust, well informed practitioner's tool box in any social work interaction. Also, in the context of this book, they are defined as 'hard' features to differentiate them from the 'softer' skills of reflection, awareness of values, emotional acuity and relationship-building which form the focus of this book. The 'hard' features might vary from situation to situation, and the reader is encouraged to think about them in relation to their own practice, and to define and understand them specifically in relation to the piece of practice which is the subject of their reflection. It is important to note that they are defined as 'hard,' not because they are in any way harsh or dogmatic, but because they are the more tangible, transparent and explicit elements of practice. As such, they contrast with the more implicit, often hidden, 'soft' features of values, emotions and the sense a social worker will make of their relationship with the service user. It is also important to be aware that reflective social work practice integrates both 'hard' and 'soft' features, so notions of binary opposites do not apply. Figure 1.1 (p. 14) should make this clear.

In recent years, much attention has been paid to the importance of the 'hard' features of practice, in relation to the emerging dominance of a managerialist approach to social work. Managerialism is a concern with the control of workers, involving overt attention to targets and measurements of performance, as well as the reliance on standardized tools and procedures to ensure 'correct' practice. As Munro (2011, p. 86) states:

> the professional account of social work practice 'in which relationships play a central role' appears to have been gradually stifled and replaced by a managerialist account that is fundamentally different. The managerialist approach has been called a 'rational-technical approach,' where the emphasis has been on the conscious, cognitive elements of the task of working with children and families, on collecting information and making plans.

The 'conscious, cognitive elements of the task' would include the transparent application of legislation, policy, procedure and theory which is essential but which, as Munro states, may 'stifle' or supplant emphasis on relationship-building if it becomes the dominant component of practice. Webb (2006, p. 21) defines rational-technical practice as an approach 'in which the practical application of knowledge is used to achieve specific, desired ends.' Once again, the 'practical application of knowledge' covers the 'hard' features of social work as already mentioned and is not concerned with reflection, values, emotions or relationships. Many writers in social work are in agreement that a 'rational-technical' approach has indeed taken hold, and that this paradigm has played out in actual social work practice, as evidenced by risk-averse practice (Fenton, 2013), the valuing of procedural knowledge over casework expertise (Whittaker, 2011), a reliance on actuarial measures of risk (Webb, 2006), an emphasis on 'measuring' outcomes in terms of key performance indicators, audit measures and a 'target driven philosophy' (Thompson and Thompson, 2008, p. 138). It can also be assumed that within a 'rational-technical approach' attention to values, emotions and, ultimately, reflective practice is undervalued.

More recently, a myriad of critiques have emerged suggesting that, for social work to be effective, it must move beyond the rational-technical practice agenda to an approach which takes far more cognizance of responsivity, reflective practice and relationship-building. Ferguson (2005, p. 781) was central in turning the rational-technical tide, with his critique of social work's 'rational-bureaucratic' responses to child deaths, characterized by highlighting changes in procedures and processes as the solution to systemic failures. His appraisal of such responses is that they ignore the emotional, psychological aspects of the work, in particular practitioners' responses to violence and their fears for themselves. He states that, within these responses, lies a view of practice as 'little more than rule following' (ibid., p. 783). Ferguson is clear that, as a profession, social work must attend to the feelings and emotions of social workers, must understand the complexities of relationship-building with sometimes very aggressive or confrontational service users, and must create organizational cultures which are reflective in nature. Only through the process of honest reflection can social workers initially identify their feelings and their progress (or lack of) in building relationships with service users. Ferguson also suggests that social work education's uncritical teaching of values, anti-oppressive practice, warmth and 'unconditional positive regard' fails to tackle the complexities in terms of values when working with families who harm their children or other involuntary service users. Workers need a way to think through properly all of the competing tensions in terms of values to deal with risk and protection, whilst still adhering to the value-base of social work. Reflective practice is the only way to do this.

The ideas in Ferguson's paper are further developed and promoted in a number of recent key policy initiatives. For example, the Munro Report (Munro, 2011) proposes changes to the child protection system in England and Wales, advocating a move away from a rational-technical system which over-emphasizes bureaucratic procedure-following, recording and targets, to one which is child-centred and characterized by social workers who are *allowed* to use their professional expertise to respond to case-by-case variations in need. The report highlights relationship-building, including the ability to ask the difficult questions, a reduction in prescriptive practice, more autonomy for social workers and an emphasis on prevention. In effect, the premise of the report is that 'when the bureaucratic aspects of work become too dominant, the heart of the work is lost' (*ibid.*, p. 10). *Changing Lives: Report of the 21st-Century Social Work Review* (Scottish Government, 2006), a wide-ranging review of social work in Scotland, recommended more autonomy for social workers and the loosening of managerial restrictions and prescriptive practice, an emphasis on the core values of social work and building relationships with service users. *Reshaping Care for Older People* (Scottish Government, 2012), again emphasizes building proper relationships with older service users and adopting a person-centred approach to finding out what the older person values and wants the outcome of any help given to be. The UK Government's white paper, *Caring for Our Future, Reforming care and Support* (Department of Health (DoH), 2012), has at its heart a commitment that 'supporting the transformation of the social work profession, we will ensure that people are confident that they will be able to develop trusting and rewarding relationships with those giving them care and support' (*ibid.*, p. 49).

The issue noted above of the need for confidence is a crucial one. Mattison (2000) notes that procedurally driven practice is attractive to workers when they feel under pressure to *act correctly*. Horwath (2007) suggests that even when a social worker feels that their actions are guided by pre-set procedures, individual subjectivities and emotions are at play in terms of choices and decisions. *Building a safe, confident future*, the Social Work Task Force report

(Department of Children, Schools and Families, 2009) noted the necessary and unavoidable balance between procedures and individual subjectivities, and pointed to the need for high-quality supervision and organizational cultures which permit and facilitate the exploration of the complexities of practice. This includes reflection on the emotional impact of the work and relationships with service users.

What all of these key policy drivers have in common is the necessity for social workers to build positive relationships with service users, whilst remaining fully aware of the complex context within which the relationships are built and sustained. Within a rational-technical framework, the relationship with the service user and engagement with the full circumstances of their life are not essential features, so it is clear that there is an impetus and aspiration in recent policy to move away from rational-technical approaches towards something quite different. In building relationships with service users, of course, attention to emotions and values via reflective practice is central.

Policy direction into action

Social work codes of practice and ethics are frameworks inside which aspiration or 'direction of travel' can be put into action. What is it that social workers need to do, and is this congruent with moving practice from rational-technical to reflective?

Currently, social work in England is regulated by the Health and Care Professions Council and is underpinned by the Professional Capabilities Framework (PCF) which sets out the required standards of professional social work practice (College of Social Work, 2012). The PCF comprises nine domains, including domain 6, 'Critical reflection and analysis,' and gives explicit attention to values, ethical principles, awareness of self and relationship building. Quite clearly, then, the PCF is congruent with the 'soft' features of practice and with a shift away from rational-technical practice.

Elsewhere in the UK, other professional bodies regulate social work practice, namely the Northern Ireland Social Care Council (NISSC, 2004), the Scottish Social Services Council (SSSC, 2004), and Cyngor Gofal Cymru/Care Council for Wales (CGC/CCW, 2004). Other than differences in title, the codes of practice issued by the regulatory bodies are the same across all three, having been developed jointly (Reamer and Shardlow, 2009). In England, the General Social Care Council (GSCC, 2004), also shared the same codes of practice until 2012, when responsibility for the regulation of social work practice was transferred to the Health and Care Professions Council as already mentioned. Consonant with the PCF, the codes of practice frame the standards of practice required from social workers. It might be expected that the 'softer' features of practice make an appearance in the codes, in that reflection, values, emotions and relationship-building must be present to move practice in the anti-rational-technical direction espoused by policy. The question is, then, do the codes indeed make reference to the 'softer' features of practice?

A critical analysis of the codes reveals that there is no mention of reflection: it is not a requirement that social workers in Northern Ireland, Wales and Scotland reflect, analyse or critically examine their practice. There are implicit allusions to relationship-building, in that workers must 'strive to establish and maintain the trust of service users and carers' by being, amongst other things, honest, trustworthy and reliable, and communicating openly (SSSC, 2004, section 2 etc.). Arguably, however, a social worker could demonstrate all of those qualities *without* working to build a relationship. There is also no mention in the codes of emotional impact or dealing with emotions. More encouragingly, values *are* a feature of the codes in that workers must treat people with dignity, respect and attention to diversity. They also must not abuse, discriminate nor misuse power. In regard to this, however, Reamer and Shardlow (2009) point out that the absence of the term 'ethics' in the title of the codes diminishes and narrows the translation of values into practice. They state that

> use of the term 'ethics' suggests that expected behaviour should be consistent with some *moral* (or values) imperatives and that the notion of *morality* is the driving force in the determination of acceptable and unacceptable behaviour ... The force of the term 'code of practice' is seemingly rather more mundane – it demands adherence as a managerial tool rather than encourages the individual practitioner (Reamer and Shardlow, 2009, np).

Reamer and Shardlow, therefore, are suggesting that, actually, the codes of practice are 'managerial' in nature (and therefore more rational-technical). Treating a person with 'respect' in a narrow, managerial way, might mean writing 'Dear Sir' on a letter, but not engaging, really listening or getting to know the person. The connection to the 'morality' of social work practice is not explicit. In contrast to this, the British Association of Social Workers' *Code of Ethics for Social Work* (British Association of Social Workers (BASW), 2012), might be expected to articulate clearly the connections between morality or values, reflection and 'soft' features of practice. Indeed, this does seem to be the case, as the code states that 'by outlining the general ethical principles, the aim is to encourage social workers across the UK to *reflect* on the challenges and dilemmas that face them and make ethically informed decisions about how to act in each particular case in accordance with the values of the profession' (BASW, 2012, p. 5). The code goes on to outline the 'values and ethical principles' which underpin the work (*ibid.*, p. 8), namely, human rights, social justice and professional integrity, then to distil from them, the 'ethical practice principles' which enact them (*ibid.*, p. 11). As already discussed, and very hearteningly, the PCF also recognizes critical reflection, the application of values, relationship-building and an endeavour for social justice as core to social work practice.

Rather than a set of managerial 'rules,' therefore, the PCF and the BASW code of ethics clearly link expected practice with the overarching values and ethical principles of social work practice. For example, social workers must 'apply the values and principles ... to their practice' (BASW, 2012, p. 11). They should also develop 'relationships based on people's rights to respect, privacy, reliability and confidentiality...' (*ibid.*, p. 12). Finally, social workers should 'strive for objectivity and self-awareness in professional practice' and 'reflect and critically evaluate their practice and be aware of their impact on others' (*ibid.*, p. 15). Clearly then, the code of ethics locate the need for reflection and the 'soft' features of practice as key elements of any social worker's responsibility and moral duty. Likewise, the *Statement of Ethical Principles* of the International Federation of Social Work (IFSW, 2013) asserts the centrality of dignity, social justice and professional integrity. In the third category, there are requirements for social workers to act with compassion and care towards the people they are working with (relationship-building), to engage in ethical debate and discussion and make ethically informed decisions (values and reflection), and to care for themselves both in personal terms and professionally (awareness of emotional impact) (*ibid.*). The individual national ethical codes of IFSW member organizations must be congruent with the overarching IFSW code, therefore supporting the argument that there is an internationally consistent requirement for social workers to be able to engage in the 'soft' features of practice. BASW, as well as the other national organizations affiliated to IFSW, are therefore congruent with the policy direction of contemporary social work in its concerted effort to move beyond a rational-technical framework for practice. It can be suggested, however, that this impetus can be somewhat lost in translation between direction and actual practice, governed by the narrower, rule-based approach to, for instance, the codes of practice in Northern Ireland, Scotland and Wales (Reamer and Shardlow, 2009).

In conclusion, this book is intended to reach beyond rational-technical, managerial and practical 'doing' agendas, including the technical application of legislation, policy, procedure and theory, to explore the underpinning 'soft' features of practice. Thus, practice, and the reflection that results, is connected to the professional morality expressed within the PCF and the BASW codes of ethics and embodied in recent policy aspiration. We will now briefly touch on the unique key themes of this book.

Key themes

There is a range of key themes that will run through this book and will become familiar touchstones when considering the role of critical reflection in social work practice. This chapter has introduced the important narratives relating to what could be described as the social work landscape. Whist this book focuses on the UK context, the recurrent themes that emerge will have a resonance internationally, as the complexity of the social work task and the need for effective critical reflection are common features of all practice contexts across all boundaries.

The balance between relationship based practice and technicist approaches

Ruch (2009) notes that relationship based models of practice have been developed from psycho-social approaches which focus on the individual within their wider context. The emphasis is on the inter- and intra-personal aspects of practice, with the relationship between practitioner and service user being of central importance. This approach to practice values the complexity that it gives rise to rather than attempting to reduce practice to a purely rational pursuit. Ward (2010, p. 185) proposes the following conditions required to underpin relationship based practice:

- Placing a premium on working with the experience and process of a helping relationship
- Attending to the emotional as well as cognitive elements for practice
- Maximizing opportunities for helpful communication
- The need for reflection at a deep level
- Focusing on the self of the worker
- An emphasis on personal qualities and values.

The conditions listed above are useful reminders of the purpose of this book. The need for the complexities and uncertainties of practice to be acknowledged and permitted is a crucial driver of the need for social workers to engage in significant reflection about their actions, motivations, emotions, values and responses in their practice.

Hennessey (2011) notes the importance of knowing one's *self* and being aware of one's emotional reactions within a social work relationship. The possession of self-knowledge allows social workers to consider the sources of their actions and reactions, and allows for the examination of the power issues inherent in care control functions of social work. This links well to the emotional awareness and regulation aspects of emotional intelligence (Salovey and Mayer, 1990). Ward (2010) notes that the term 'self' is a complex one insofar as it involves one's beliefs, experiences and values, but is not a fixed entity. By this Ward means that our 'self' will change and fluctuate over time and from context to context. This reminds us that a relationship-based approach is contextual and professionally orientated rather than neutral and fixed. Munro (2011) acknowledges the need for practitioners to receive supervision that allows them to consider the emotional content of practice and the way that this stream of information for practitioners interfaces with concrete knowledge and procedures. Simply put, when social work is seen through this lens, then the full richness of practice with all its attendant complexities and unpredictability must be explored and appreciated.

The relationship based conception of social work is often pitted against more procedural and bureaucratic conceptions. If the procedural conception of practice is taken to its extreme, then the process of practice can be reduced to following a set of instructions without any consideration of the aforementioned complexities and unpredictability. Ferguson (2005), as already discussed, noted that the reality of practice in relation to child protection was such that workers felt they had no opportunities to explore and articulate the complexities of working in an environment of fear and aggression, and that this was in part due to the rigidity of processes and procedures. If the relationship aspects of social work were removed (or, more likely, repressed) then there would not be a need for this book; social work practice, supervision and outcomes would be containable within a linear and procedural framework. As evidenced earlier in this chapter, this is not supported by the ethical codes, policies and narratives of the profession in the twenty-first century.

A key driver of this book is the acknowledgement that social work as a profession continues to seek clarity about its purpose and place within the wider political and inter-professional landscape. Howe (2008) forcefully advocated that the knowledge and roles that underpin the social work task are only relevant in the context of the skills and relationships that the social worker possesses and develops. Sudberry (2002) concurs with this when she notes that the establishment and maintenance of a positive and trusting relationship with service users is required before any of the more tangible outcomes-based benefits of social work can occur. This is a powerful point in that it shows the dynamic and fluid complexities of relationships as being the catalyst and environment for the rational-technical aspects of practice to emerge, rather than being viewed as a marginalized aspect of practice.

Although relationship-based social work with service users is at the heart of this book, it would be remiss to ignore the other relationships which abound in contemporary, multi-disciplinary social work practice. These relationships are also fundamental to critically reflective practice, characterized as they often are by different viewpoints, different values, different perceptions of status and complex communication strategies. Subsequent chapters deal with these issues and relate them to specific social work contexts.

Emotions and social work practice

Throughout this book, we will refer to the emotional aspects of social work practice and the need for social workers to engage in critical reflection which explores and articulates these aspects. It is important that we clarify what is meant by 'emotions' at this stage in the book to make subsequent references to them relevant and useful.

The study of human emotions has attracted a great deal of debate about their nature, purpose and uses. The purpose of this book is not to resolve the complexities of this vast area of research and inquiry, but rather to assist the reader in the development of a clear sense of the key aspects of the construct.

Oatley (2004) describes emotions as responses to a range of stimuli that trigger both cognitive and physiological reactions. This view of emotions helpfully unites two key (and at times) opposing strands of emotions. The seminal work of William James (1890) placed emphasis on emotions requiring 'an object' to respond to. This could be an event, a physical object or simply a thought. His conception however was rooted in the *physiological* reaction this might incur (i.e. the emotion of fear may incur breathlessness) and as such suggests that emotions are simply experienced. Lazarus (1991) noted that there are *cognitive* processes at play in terms of our appraisal of situations and indeed the labelling of our emotions. The idea that the initial physiological emotional response is then followed quickly by a cognitive judgement is backed up persuasively by the work of neuroscientists such as Damasio (1994) and LeDoux (1997) who observed that damage to the amygdala and/or the neocortex areas of the brain can impair the ability to control and/or articulate emotional responses. Barrett (2012) pulls these strands together inside a broad conceptual framework of emotions, and notes that the physiological, neurological and cognitive aspects of emotions must also be located within a socially constructed sphere.

What this area of research highlights is that emotions can be felt *and* thought about. They can be triggered by our interaction within situations, and occur when our goals are impeded or facilitated (Lazarus, 1991). This thinking laid the foundation for the rise of concepts such as emotional intelligence. Simply put, emotional intelligence is the ability to identify and manage emotional responses within oneself and in others (Salovey and Mayer, 1990). Ingram (2013) identifies the cogent links between such a view of emotions with key characteristics of social workers (empathy, warmth, transparency and genuineness) and goes on to highlight the overlaps between emotional self-knowledge and reflection. The complexity of understanding the sources and impact of one's emotions (both conscious and unconscious) necessitate the active pursuit of opportunities for critical reflection. It is also worth noting at this point that social workers will experience emotions within a context of their professional role, and this book will also cast a light on the socially constructed nature of emotions (Turner and Stets, 2005) and in turn upon their expression and presence in practice.

Values and social work practice

Another key theme of the book is the recognition that values are absolutely central to social work practice. As documented by a significant number of authors, the advancement of a rational-technical, managerial and neoliberal approach to social work has contributed to an erosion of social work values. For example, Jones (2001) found that social work departments were described as grim places to work, populated by disillusioned and unhappy social workers. The roots of the workers' unhappiness lay in the reduction of their jobs to gate-keeping, having little time for getting to know service users, and an inability to help when they felt help was required. In other words, workers were struggling to base their expected work practices upon the values supposedly espoused at the centre of their profession. Preston-Shoot (2003) found similar themes in his review of the evidence from social work practitioners. Social workers reported 'demoralisation and disillusionment' because they felt 'unable to uphold the knowledge base and values of a competent professional' (Preston-Shoot, 2003, p. 10). Echoing Jones' findings, workers reported a lack of time to build relationships with service-users, and an over-reliance on procedures and routines, leading to an inability to achieve value-based practice.

Di Franks (2008) proposed the concept of 'disjuncture,' that is, the ethical stress experienced by workers when they cannot base their practice upon their values (as above). There is a persuasive body of literature (for example, Taylor, 2007; O'Donnell et al., 2008; Calderwood et al., 2009; Fenton, 2013) pointing to the importance and power of workers' feelings of 'disjuncture', including increased staff turnover, the impact on disjuncture of risk aversion, the long-term corrosive effects of disjuncture, the impact on job satisfaction and the consequent inability of workers experiencing disjuncture to take moral action. The authors feel that disjuncture is a key concept, because recognition and understanding of it and its associated feelings can lead to further critical reflection on the issues and, hopefully, moral action in terms of redress. Kosny and Eakin (2008) undertook a study in three not-for-profit agencies in Canada and found that disjuncture was minimal in the studies they undertook, because workers could base their practices firmly upon their values. Workers were encouraged to 'muck in,' to see the service users as suffering the effects of an unfair society (social work's commitment to social justice in action), to view boundaries as permeable and to do their utmost to help. Of course, this is not to suggest that social work is quite as simple or straightforward as that, but it does illuminate the necessity for social workers to recognize, reflect upon and analyse any gap which arises between values and practice.

Once again, then, there is a clear need for workers to find opportunities for critical reflection. Without critical reflection, the explicit recognition of values, the understanding of feelings of disjuncture and the analysis of the feeling will remain unexplored.

The Reflective Social Work Practitioner Model

Chapter 2 more fully explores the concepts and meanings of reflection, critical reflection and reflexivity, but it can be surmised from the preceding discussion that critical reflection is the *process* required for a social worker to fully understand, recognize, accept and use the emotional content, the understanding of the relationship with the service user and the level of value–practice congruence or incongruence in any practice situation. We argue that without these 'soft' features of practice, social work is in danger of becoming wholly characterized by rational-technical, bureaucratic and managerial processes. As outlined previously, relationship-based social work is the antithesis of a rational-technical model, and therefore is fundamental in helping a worker withstand the technical excesses of managerialism.

Hopefully, readers will now understand the evolution and development of the model (Figure 1.1) and will see why we feel it is applicable to social work practice. The 'hard' features of practice, as already discussed, are placed in an outer ring of the model, but that does not imply they are unimportant. Quite the contrary: legislation, policy, procedures and theory are 'givens' in any practice situation. The figure, however, illustrates that the focus of this book is deliberately concerned with the 'soft,' less tangible features of practice. It is relatively easy to talk about the application of the 'soft' features in the abstract, but perhaps more difficult to tease them out and articulate them as is required by reflective practice in 'real' situations. Therefore, the following chapters will all end with the application of the model to a practice situation, to assist the

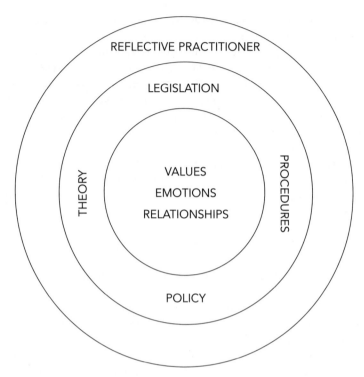

Figure 1.1 The Reflective Social Work Practitioner Model

reader in practising reflective social work, with purposeful attention to the 'soft' features above.

How to use this book

As has been discussed in this chapter, the working life of a social worker is full of complexities, challenges, opportunities and uncertainties. Our profession has a keen awareness of the profundity of the impact that interventions and decisions associated with our role can have on the lives of the service users with whom we work. The importance of social workers critically reflecting upon their actions and the way in which they as individuals construct and interpret the content and experience of their practice, has been highlighted, and it is this focus on the individual within their wider personal and professional contexts that is crucial for this book's usefulness to its readers. Chapter 2 will expand on how social work practitioners might understand, and practice, in critically reflective and reflexive ways.

Each chapter is built around the working week of a range of social workers. The diary format is designed to bring to life the competing and varied demands on a social worker that drive the need to engage in critical reflection. We hope that the reader will be able to map these chapters against their own diaries, and consider the issues discussed here more easily in relation to their own context. In conjunction with these diary excerpts, case scenarios have been constructed which link to the chapter topics and demonstrate how the critically reflective process in relation to the chapter topic can be followed.

Ultimately however, this book is intended to become a useful companion to practice, studies and professional development. The suggested tasks and activities are designed to bridge the gap between the content of the book and the specifics of the reader's personal and professional lives. This book will be a resource which can be returned to frequently in professional work and studies, as the reflective and reflexive processes proposed within are by definition ever-evolving and ongoing. It purposely highlights a broad range of service contexts to underline the universality of its content and to resonate across the whole profession.

A guide to the chapters

This book is intended to take the reader through a broad range of contexts and experiences that social workers may encounter within their working lives. We briefly introduce here the contents and purpose of each chapter to map the terrain that will be covered.

Chapter 2 explores the concepts of reflection and reflexivity further, incorporating the development of thinking around reflection and its contemporary position in social work practice. This chapter will clarify concepts for the reader before we embark on the more applied chapters that follow.

Chapter 3 deals with the ways that social workers engage and communicate with people, sometimes in difficult circumstances. The need for reflection 'in' and 'on' such interactions will be explored.

Chapters 4 and 5 are linked, and concerned with assessment and intervention. There is a particular focus on the negative impact of prescriptive, process-driven practice and the value of 'helping' within any social work intervention. The complexities therein are explored via reflection and analysis, and the sense of the personal and professional domain of the social worker is highlighted.

Chapter 6 focuses on making risk decisions and includes the balancing of rights with risks. The reflective activities invite complex 'risk-sensible' thinking, and the central concern is the need to achieve anti-oppressive practice.

Chapter 7 investigates the intricate dynamics surrounding social work practice in meetings. These powerful dynamics and resultant emotions and behaviour are analysed, and readers are encouraged to use their own experience to reflect upon, and make sense, of the 'hidden' processes which happen in meetings.

Chapter 8 explores the written articulation of practice across a range of formats. It examines research findings which suggest that the 'soft' elements of practice are less evident in written accounts of practice, and considers suggestions for heightening the role and profile of reflection in this area.

Chapter 9 considers the place and importance of supervision in social work, with particular attention to the helpful and unhelpful elements of supervision. A model of co-created reflective supervision is proposed.

Chapter 10 brings together the key messages from this book and indicates how these messages can be taken forward into practice to contribute to the development of a reflective social work organization.

This book can be used as a companion to practice, as it is both practical in format, *and* designed to elicit complex reflective thinking around the practical examples. We hope that the reader finds it both useful and enjoyable.

Further resources

Munro, E. (2011) *The Munro Review of Child Protection: Final Report.*
Current thinking on the role of relationships, emotions and values in child protection.

Hennessey, R. (2011) *Relationship Skills in Social Work.*
Puts relationships at the heart of social work.

CHAPTER 2

Dynamics of critical reflection and reflexivity

In the previous chapter, when discussing the social work context, the reader was introduced to the 'hard' and 'soft' features of social work practice. This chapter will introduce the reader to critical reflection and reflexivity with the purpose of developing the 'soft' aspects of social work practice. It will be developed through the following key themes:

* Key definitions and models of reflection and critical reflection
* Key aspects of critical reflection
* Methods of undertaking critical reflection
* Key aspects of reflexivity.

Critical reflection

Reflection is the process of considering events or situations to understand beyond *what happened* to *why it happened* and how different people within that context *might have felt* about it (Bolton, 2010). After a systematic review of literature, White, Fook, and Gardner (2006) found that authors have defined reflection differently depending on their theoretical approach. They suggest that, overall, reflection involves a process of examining one's assumptions, understanding the basis of those assumptions leading to a re-examination of them in a particular context, followed by a review of practice. *Reflective practice* is the application of this reflection to modify one's practice.

Argyris and Schön (1974) proposed models of single-loop and double-loop learning which link up well with the way that social workers might undertake reflection and reflective practice. In Chapter 1, the reader was introduced to the rational-technical approach. When seen in the context of reflection, this technical approach might lead to single-loop learning. For example, if something goes wrong in day-to-day practice, the social worker might 'reflect' on what happened, and stop at the view that 'I did

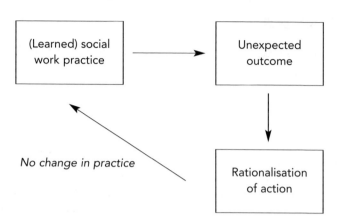

Figure 2.1 Single-loop rational-technical practice. *Source*: adapted from Redmond (2006).

everything according to the legislation and procedure, therefore if things did not work out, it is not my fault. It might be that this service user does not understand how things are done'. Figure 2.1 illustrates the process of single-loop thinking.

This single-loop way of learning is seen to be the most basic form of reflection. Box 2.1 highlights what reflective recording might look like when the social worker engages in a single loop only.

Box 2.1: Example of single-loop reflection

There had been difficulties getting the family to engage with the social work team, so I did an unannounced visit in order to try and catch them at home and ask them why they were not co-operating. When I arrived at the house it was obvious someone was in so I was persistent and eventually I was allowed in. I spoke with Sally and she told me she didn't want to work with the social work department because she was afraid she would have her children taken away.

Reflecting on this I recognize people may be fearful of social work involvement but there are statutory responsibilities to ensure that children are safe. I feel confident using my statutory power in this way and would do so again in future.

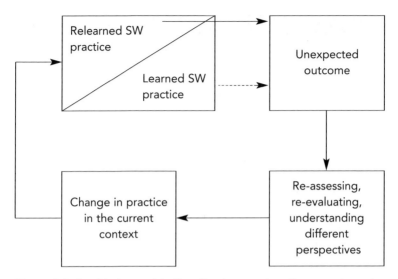

Figure 2.2 Double-loop critically reflective practice. *Source:* adapted from Redmond (2006).

In critiquing this, however, in our view, after reflection there should be some learning leading to change and, hopefully, resulting in improved practice. Therefore, the reader is advised to move into a double loop, where the outcome leads to a reassessment of what happened as a result of understanding events from the perspective of others (Figure 2.2). Heron (2005) suggests that within social work, critical reflection helps in understanding how one is socially located and how the social worker can challenge power dynamics in their encounters with service users, thus creating an anti-oppressive practice.

This requires that the social worker acts as an individual who is cognitively flexible and willing to learn from every action and outcome. Box 2.2 provides an example of what the reflective recording emerging from double-loop learning might look like.

It is important to note that the unexpected outcome shown in Figures 2.1 and 2.2 does not have to be negative. It can be a positive outcome which will help in building on what went well to enhance effective practice. This will also be considered to be double-loop learning.

Box 2.2: Example of double-loop reflection

Reflecting on my visit to Sally I realize that her anxiety about involvement from a statutory social worker was creating a barrier to communication and engagement with her. With this in mind I approached my discussion with Sally from the perspective of support, focussing on Sally's strong bonds with her children and how she had the capacity to bring about changes in her life.

I feel my positive approach was pivotal in helping Sally feel she could work with me. I am conscious of the statutory responsibility to ensure Sally's children are safe and protected. However, I can also see that, as I become more experienced, I feel less inclined to start with the procedural perspective which may simply be because I understand it more and so feel more comfortable with what I can and can't do. This has freed me up to rely much more on my emotions and my use of emotional intelligence.

I know making an unannounced visit was important in this case. However, I was a bit uncomfortable with regards to exerting my power in this way and forcing myself on the family. Was it ethical? I also wonder what impact this might have on my relationship with Sally. I need to be mindful of this in future interactions with her and any other family.

Key aspects of critical reflection

After a review of other authors' views about critically reflective practice, White et al. (2006) have identified eight key aspects:

1. Awareness of underlying assumptions
2. Value of experiential learning
3. Understanding of different perspectives (no one reality)
4. Ability to deconstruct dominant discourses
5. Awareness of the impact of social/political context on self and practice
6. Ability to understand and challenge power dynamics
7. Awareness of one's reflexivity
8. Personal or organizational change.

Therefore, to become critically reflective, social workers have to go beyond a procedural rational-technical approach to their practice. This requires not only the ability to be critically analytical of an incident and the emotions of the main actors; the social worker also needs to be able to draw upon an ability to understand different perspectives and value them, alongside a readiness to deconstruct and challenge dominant views and inherent power dynamics. It is important to remember that this reflective practice, which involves softer features of emotions and values, is not happening in a vacuum; social workers need to be mindful of their interaction with the equally important 'hard' features such as legislation, theory, procedures and organizational or national policy (see Figure 1.1).

For a social worker to be an effective critically reflective practitioner, it is important that there is an organizational culture that is supportive and provides a safe environment. Park and Millora (2012) found that reflection was a negative predictor of 'psychological well-being' owing to its focus on negative experiences and the deconstruction of prior simplistic ways of knowing practice and the social world. Where there is not a safe environment, the social worker may revert to a rational-technical approach. This would be unfortunate as, in an empirical study conducted in the USA involving 14,527 full time college students, Park and Millora (2012) found that reflection was the strongest predictor of 'ethical caring' (commitment to helping others through activities such as promoting racial understanding, engaging with the community, etc.), followed by 'leadership'.

Models of reflection

Several models of reflection have been proposed over the last four decades. Some of them are summarized in Table 2.1 and show a development over time, from quite simple ones in the 1970s and 1980s to more sophisticated models in recent times. It can be seen that there is a shift from cyclical models to the list type of model, although these models have been extended with probing questions. Models that have phases or sections have come to the fore recently, as they can show progress over time or can be used at different times depending on the practitioner's experience.

The list type of model tends to build on Borton's (1970) three questions: *What?, So What?, Now What?* These questions provide a list framework enabling the social worker to focus on the issue, what it means to them, and how they are going to respond. It is a useful model in the beginning stages of reflection as it is straight forward to understand and complete. This is likely to lead the practitioner towards reflecting on their own self and their practice but

Table 2.1 Analysis of models of reflection

Author	Title	Type of Model	Features
Borton (1970)	Borton's Framework Guiding Reflective Activities	List	Reflection on action
Schon (1983, 1987)	Reflection in Action Reflection on Action	Phased	Reflecting both 'in' and 'on' practice
Kolb (1984)	Kolb's Learning Cycle	Cyclical	Reflection on action
Gibbs (1988)	Gibbs Reflective Cycle	Cyclical	Focus on emotions
Atkins and Murphy (1994)	Atkins and Murphy's Model of Reflection	Cyclical	Includes questions about emotion and knowledge
Johns (1994)	Johns' Model of Structured Reflection	List	Structured – makes explicit the knowledge that we use in practice
Crisp, Lister and Dutton, (2005)	Critical Incident Analysis	Critical incident analysis	Reflecting on a specific incident
Fook and Gardner (2007)	Critical Reflection Framework	Phased	Holistic model used in an ethical learning climate
Lay and McGuire (2010)	DEAL Model	List with questions	Questions that focus on critical reflection
Taylor (2010)	REFLECT Model	Phased	Holistic approach to reflection

is unlikely to enable an inexperienced reflector to think critically about their practice.

The models that have adapted Borton's construct by adding extra stages or questions can be more successful in encouraging criticality in the social worker's reflection. For instance, Johns' (1994) model, which was designed to be used in a guided reflection process, encourages the practitioner to think about the knowledge that informed them. This brings the worker to think about the theory that can impact on practice and which informs their praxis.

Another list-type model that extends practice is the Lay and McGuire (2010) DEAL, which has three main elements: *Describe*, *Examine* and *Articulate Learning*. Additionally it employs critical thinking questions which the worker can use to deepen their reflections. DEAL is a tool that can help social workers to critically analyse their practice.

The cyclical models are dynamic and very useful as they incorporate action. Kolb's (1984) learning cycle is the most well-known of the cyclical models but has limitations due to its simplicity. However, Gibbs (1988) and Atkins and Murphy (1994) have developed their cyclical model to include discussion around emotions and their impact, and, in Atkins and Murphy's (1994) case, a more complex analysis of feelings and the relevance of knowledge that is linked to action.

However, none of the models discussed above explicitly ask practitioners to question their assumptions about the event that they are reflecting upon, though, of course, reflecting on their own emotions and knowledge may lead a social worker to question their assumptions. As White et al. (2006, p. 12) espouse critical reflection to be:

> the process by which adults identify the assumptions that govern their action, locate the historical and cultural origins of the assumptions, question the meaning of the assumptions, and develop alternative ways of acting

Fook and Gardner's (2007) Critical Reflection Framework is a phased process where this kind of questioning can be undertaken. Their model, which is designed to be used in a safe learning environment, utilizes critical incidents while challenging underlying assumptions with the purpose of reformulating students practice paradigm. Phased models such as Fook and Gardner's (2007) and Taylor's (2010) REFLECT model (Readiness, Exercising thought, Following systematic processes, Leaving oneself open to answers,

Enfolding insights, Changing awareness, Tenacity in maintaining reflection) are purposely holistic so that they can be utilized when and where a practitioner is placed to use them.

Another phased model is Shaw's (2013), which illustrates the journey that social workers may take in developing their reflective skills. The centre of the model represents the very beginning of a worker's journey, where they may know very little about reflection and are aware that it takes time to develop reflective skills. Once these skills of questioning have developed over time, a social worker is well placed to begin questioning the political, social, cultural as well as the emotional and personal elements of practice. This enables social workers to find the strength and moral focus to act as critically reflective practitioners in this age of bureaucratic, rational-technical practice.

Another model worth expanding on is Schon's (1983, 1987) conceptualization of reflection-in-action and reflection-on-action. Schon sees the former as reflecting in the midst of action and the latter as reflection after the action or event is over. Thompson and Thompson (2008) have built on this to suggest reflection-for-action, which includes planning and preparing for future action or potential consequences.

Methods of reflection

Different models of reflection lead to different ways of undertaking reflection. Most of the models are based on the assumption that reflective recording will be undertaken. Recording might be in the form of written entries or audio/video recordings. Reflective recordings can be maintained as a part of the social worker's portfolio (e-portfolios), professional diaries, case notes or through the use of audio/video digital recorders (see Chapter 8 to consider ways of bringing reflection to your practice recordings).

Recording of reflection serves several functions:

- Revisiting reflective recording at a later date:
  o Leads to reflection on previous reflections which might help in coming up with a solution for a current situation
  o Leads to deeper level of reflection due to other experiences since the recording, as well as the ability to stand back and look at the same incident differently.
- The social worker can involve a critical friend to challenge their reflections in a constructive manner. This may help in

Reflective Activity 2.1

Search the web for examples of reflective journals. You might find this website useful as a starting point:

http://www.deakin.edu.au/itl/assets/resources/pd/tl-modules/teaching-approach/group-assignments/learning-journals.pdf

You might want to consider Bassot, B. (2013) *The Reflective Journal* (Basingstoke: Palgrave Macmillan) – a structured but flexible journal that you can use.

reflecting more deeply due to the questions the critical friend may pose and/or help to motivate the social worker, who might be being too hard on themselves.

Due to the sensitive and confidential nature of social work practice, it is important that no identifiers (e.g., name or characteristics of the service users) are used in any form of reflective recording or conversations. Similarly, the use of videos is limited to situations where such recording is permitted and will not cause concern to the service user. It is important to consider some examples of such reflective recordings (see Reflective Activity 2.1).

Over the years, as the reader goes on a reflective journey, they might find that they move from writing descriptively (Box 2.1) to being able to write in a more critically reflective manner (Box 2.2). Park and Millora (2012) found that the strength of reflection as a predictor of ethical caring and leadership increased for those in third year of study, highlighting that students had learned to become more reflective over a period of time. This was as a result of engaging in greater levels of self-reflection and attending more classes with aspects of reflective writing or journal keeping. Jindal-Snape and Holmes (2009) in their longitudinal study, in which they followed participants over a year, found that all the participants, as students and then as practitioners in a caring profession similar to social work, considered reflection to be crucial and had found ways of embedding it in their practice. However, the main difference for them had come in the ways in which they recorded and undertook reflection. There was a shift from keeping a reflective diary (which was a course requirement) to more spontaneous reflections through conversations with colleagues, support and supervision and through case notes.

One example from the study:

case-notes – a brief description and outcome of reflection is recorded. Actually reflections are recorded, for example 'I don't feel I'd dealt with this ... didn't feel this went that well ... will discuss with ...'. These reflections in case notes are brief and help to get clarity of purpose of what I'm doing and what's needed. (Jindal-Snape and Holmes, 2009, p. 225)

However, not every social worker might find reflective recordings to be the most useful method for undertaking reflection. Some might prefer a conversation and reflective dialogue with a colleague. For example, one of the practitioners in Jindal-Snape and Holmes (2009, p. 224) study said that:

Diary was ... you are only going to be as good as your own thought. Unless you have a Eureka moment! You need other people to build or challenge. Social process is important. When you are immersed or troubled, they make light of it and remind you of ... theories or challenge your ... theories.

Conversational reflection with peers in the Service ... I find this most helpful as it allows you a safer space to reflect fully. It is also most reassuring as you feel less alone ... I find it very effective as I gain both support and reflection from the process of peer support.

These quotes highlight that the dynamic social process of reflecting with others can be quite important. This emphasizes the importance of support networks for those undertaking reflections, for example by staff they work with. For example, some newly qualified practitioners highlighted this in Jindal-Snape and Holmes (2009, p. 224):

My only concern with reflection is the paralysis of analysis. It is a fine balance. You have to reflect, peel back the layers of onion and need to pull back especially if there is an emotive element ... peer reflection is helpful [as] it may inject humour into it.

In the case of social workers, this would translate to support through supervision (see Chapter 9) as well as through group reflection processes. Also, it is worth noting that as students/ practitioners, one should try to finish reflections on a positive note, which in some cases might be 'what should I do the next time?'

Therefore, reflective processes might involve reflective recording or conversation or both. Various techniques can be used as part of the reflection process and reflective exercises which the reader might want to try when they move to other chapters:

1. **Writing**
   Moon (1999, 2004) has suggested several techniques for reflective writing, such as double-entry journals (self or with others), free narrative, lists, lists followed by narratives, metaphors, mind maps, photographs, poems, responding to 'What?, How?, Why?, So what?' questions, sketches, stepping stones to list events/incidents chronologically, stories, SWOT (Strength, Weakness, Opportunity and Threat) analysis, unsent letters, writing from different angles (practitioner, service user).

2. **Conversation**
   Some practitioners prefer reflective conversations, These could be generated through creative drama with peers, team reflection, formal peer support arrangements, personal support arrangements, informal peer support arrangements, formal supervision arrangements.

3. **Audio**
   Some practitioners find it easier to audio record their reflection. It is beneficial to record reflections immediately after the event and then return to the audio for the next cycle of reflection.

4. **Video**
   Similarly, videoing an event or reflective dialogue can be effective technique for undertaking and recording reflection. For example, you can video the supervision meeting, interaction with peers, or yourself reflecting about a case; followed by a return to the video for the next cycle of reflection.

Usually one would use several of these methods in combination, such as writing and conversation with supervisor. Further, within the same method the reflective exercises can be carried out using a combination of ways of undertaking them. For example, stepping stones can be used as a reminder of the chronological sequence of events, i.e. to capture the details and the descriptive aspect of *what* happened. This can be followed by a free narrative in which the focus can be on critical reflection of *why* something might have happened and the *so what* to plan the next steps (for example, What?, So what?, Now what? discussed earlier).

To reiterate, it is important to ensure confidentiality. Therefore, social workers might find it useful to use fictionalized stories or poems. Similarly, creative drama can be used to provide that fictional aspect alongside being able to reflect from different perspectives with a group of peers. Reflective Activity 2.2 uses a photograph as a springboard for reflection which can be undertaken individually or as part of a group reflection activity.

Some might find using a photograph useful to project their feelings about a particular incident. It is important to remember that the same photograph will resonate differently with different people. For example, one social worker might concentrate on the child at risk; another might focus on being well supported by the ropes; whilst another might make a comment on soaring higher than the buildings. Some of this imagery might readily come through metaphors, for example, 'hanging by the rope', 'too much

Reflective Activity 2.2

1. Consider this photograph in the context of your social work practice. What resonates with you? Why is that?
2. Write about this in a reflective journal or diary using at least one of the techniques mentioned earlier.

of a rope to hang yourself on', 'weakest links' or 'flying high' or 'social worker supporting the child to achieve his potential'. Some social workers might prefer a double-entry journal. This requires the practitioner to write on the right hand page, leaving the left hand page blank, either for the practitioner to go back after a few days to reflect on their own reflection, or for a critical friend to critique their reflection and leave questions for them to further reflect on. The latter style is a way of reflecting with others without having to do it face to face, which might be problematic for a busy social worker. A mind map can be used to effectively peel back layers of what happened and then respond to 'why' questions as much as possible. This can then be used to structure reflective and reflexive writing and/or dialogue.

Reflexivity

Jindal-Snape and Hannah (2014) have defined reflexivity as the ability to understand where one is coming from and how one's perspective is influenced by one's values, beliefs, cultural norms and life experiences. It is about examining how and why, without conscious thought, one might have created structures and practices which might be against one's espoused values (Bolton, 2010). Fook and Gardner (2007) have defined reflexivity as the ability to be able to see what we might not normally see, such as our social and historical context, others' perspectives, and the impact of our interactions, and the ways in which these can reinforce unequal social relationships or hierarchies of professional power. Reflexivity requires that the social worker can deal with uncertainty and is willing to change deeply held views and assumptions (Bolton, 2010).

Reflexivity comes about as a consequence of critical reflection and movement into deeper levels of understanding of what lies behind an action or thought. Shaw's (2013) model goes some way to explain how reflexivity can be developed through critical reflection and the examination of social structures. To understand the difference between reflection and reflexivity, consider the questions social workers might ask themselves in the context of an incident (see Box 2.3).

The questions in Box 2.3 indicate that reflexivity involves peeling off further layers to understand the influence of one's 'self' on one's behaviour, requiring a good understanding of one's values

Box 2.3: Questions to prompt reflection and reflexivity

Questions for critical reflection

What happened?
Why did it happen?
How was I feeling?
What were my assumptions?
What informed these assumptions?
What needs to change?
What can I do next time?

Questions for reflexivity

How did I influence what happened?
Why did I behave in that way?
Why might I have *felt* the way I did during the situation, and now, when reflecting on it?
How has who I am affected my view of what happened, my values, opportunities and life choices, and subsequently my reflection?
What beliefs or ways of challenging my assumptions will allow me to look at this from others' perspectives?

and emotions, and how these play out in interpersonal relationships. Further, a reflexive social worker will be able to understand what influenced their values and the way they felt in a particular situation.

This can be made clearer by looking at how the reader might be able to bring reflexivity into reflective writing that they have already undertaken. Box 2.4 uses the reflective recording from Box 2.2 to highlight the type of questions that the social workers can ask themselves to become more reflexive. These questions are in bold and italics.

At this point the reader might want to refer back to the Reflective Social Work Practitioner Model (Figure 1.1). It will also be useful to understand this by considering a case study.

Reflective and reflexive questioning of Belaku's actions and emotions might provide a better understanding of what was happening.

The deeper one can go to unpack one's understanding of professionalism, or the emotions generated in a particular context, the more reflexive one will be able to become. In terms of emotions, it

Box 2.4: Example of questions to deepen critical reflection to move towards reflexivity

Reflecting on my visit to Sally I realize that her anxiety about involvement from a statutory social worker was creating a barrier to communication and engagement with her. *Did I do anything on the day that might have led to her anxiety? Did I identify her emotions accurately? Why did I think she was anxious? Did she say that or was it my assumption?* With this in mind I approached my discussion with Sally from the perspective of support, focussing on Sally's strong bonds with her children and how she had the capacity to bring about changes in her life. *Why do I think that Sally has strong bonds with her children? What do 'strong bonds' mean to me? Why? Is my understanding based on theories of attachment and resilience? Or is it based on my values and life experiences? Would they mean the same for others? What makes me think that Sally wants to make a change to her life? Is this her wish or my expectation?*

I feel my positive approach was pivotal in helping Sally feel she could work with me. *Why do I feel my approach was positive? Did Sally think it was positive?* I am conscious of the statutory responsibility to ensure Sally's children are safe and protected. *Am I clear about the procedures? Am I acting in the best interest of Sally, her children, the entire family or my organization? Why?* However, I can also see that, as I become more experienced, I feel less inclined to start with the procedural perspective which may simply be because I understand it more and so feel more comfortable with what I can and can't do. *Why is that? Is that influenced by my own personal experiences and/or my value base? Is it influenced my recent readings?* This has freed me up to rely much more on my emotions and my use of emotional intelligence. *How comfortable am I relying on my emotions? Has this changed for me? When and why?*

I know making an unannounced visit was important in this case. *Why do I think so?* However, I was a bit uncomfortable with regards to exerting my power in this way and forcing myself on the family. Was it ethical? *Why was I uncomfortable? Was there a clash between my personal and professional values? How did I deal with my own emotions? Did my discomfort have any impact on my interaction with Sally?* I also wonder what impact this might have on my relationship with Sally. *Do I need to do further reading*

> *around issues of trust and power dynamics?* I need to be mindful of this in future interactions with her and any other family. *What have I learned from this situation? How can I apply it to future situations? Is it something worth discussing with colleagues and supervisor?*

Case Study 2.1

Belaku is a social worker based in a local authority, who primarily works with children and families who are asylum seekers. In a team meeting with other professionals he gets very upset and cries when outlining one of his cases where a 6-year-old child had suffered what he considered to be horrific abuse prior to moving to the host country. He feels embarrassed and concerned that his colleagues would think he was not being professional.

Reflective Activity 2.3

1. Why do you think Belaku is feeling that he has acted in an unprofessional manner? What do you think Belaku's understanding of being a professional is? Why might he be thinking that? Why do *you* think that?
2. Construct a 5-minute presentation (oral or written) for a secondary school careers day that you have been invited to. Within that, consider how you will explain to young people what being a professional social worker *is*. What informed your thinking for this presentation? What is your understanding of being a professional? Please consider written and unwritten messages you might have received throughout your professional training and practice, as well as your life experiences to date.
3. Think of an incident when you were emotionally affected by one of the cases you were working on. Try to unpack why you might have been feeling in that way. You might want to use some of the questions for reflexivity mentioned earlier.

is possible that Belaku had similar experiences at that age. Or that he has a 6-year-old child and his multiple identities as a father and social worker came together in that situation. Or it could be that his value base makes him strongly believe in children's rights and he sees this event as an impingement of that, with no control over what happened.

Similarly, in terms of professionalism, he might have an image of a professional who can work calmly without being affected by what is happening in the life of the service user. This image might have come through his professional training or from elsewhere. If Belaku were to engage in critical reflection and reflexivity, he might start considering the origin of this. He might remember that when he was 10 years old there was a fire in his neighbourhood. The fire fighters and paramedics, whom he saw as professionals, were on the scene and appeared to be doing their work calmly despite what was happening around them. It is possible that in a supervision session he was advised not to get too emotionally involved in the lives of his clients as it might lead to him being 'burned out' soon. Once he is aware of what gives him his ideas of what professionalism is, or why this case might have affected him, he can start understanding his emotions as well as managing them effectively. He might then see emotions as a healthy part of his practice. Also, he might then be able to bring about a change in others' perception of professionalism and emotional attachment to the service users.

Therefore, reflexivity might involve standing back and peeling layers and layers of reasons, delving deeply into the reasons behind one's actions and thoughts. It can be uncomfortable as one might have to deal with incidents that were traumatic or difficult to understand from the new world-view that the social worker might now have. It might be beneficial to engage in this process with a critical friend or a trustworthy colleague. Chapter 9 will pick this idea again in the context of support and supervision.

Conclusion

Reflection and reflexivity are seen to be the 'soft' features of the Reflective Social Work Practitioner Model (see Chapter 1). However, especially in the context of critical reflection, the social worker needs to be aware of the 'hard' features and their influence on practice. Further, reflexivity reminds the reader to be aware of the social worker's interaction with both the 'hard' and 'soft' features, and how *they* might influence these features. Readers are encouraged to apply their understanding of reflection and reflexivity to their practice as well as to activities included in Chapters 3 to 9.

Further resources

Bassot, B. (2013) *The Reflective Journal*.
Takes the reader through a systematic journey to becoming a critically reflective practitioner by providing theory and reflective activities.

Fook, J., and Gardner, F. (2007) *Practising Critical Reflection*.
Provides further insight into significance and models of reflection.

Moon, J. (2004) *A Handbook of Reflective and Experiential Learning: Theory and Practice*.
Provides more information about reflective exercises and gives some good examples of reflective recordings.

Thorsen, C.A., and DeVore, S. (2012) 'Analysing reflection on/for action: A new approach', *Reflective Practice: International and Multidisciplinary Perspectives*, 14(1), 88–103.
Helpful for further information about conceptualization and models of reflection.

CHAPTER 3

Communication skills for building and sustaining relationships

Social work communication takes place in a range of contexts and with a range of individuals, although this chapter will focus purely on the relationships indicated in the case study. It will develop the ideas explored in the preceding chapters by applying them in the context of social work communication and by linking them to a case study. The key themes of this chapter, which are transferable across a range of contexts, are listed below:

- Reflection and the use of skills
- A framework for reflecting upon communication in practice
- Working with resistance

Aileen's diary (Education Social Worker)

Monday
10.00 *Referral team meeting*
11.00 *Letters and phone calls re new referrals*
2.00 *Home visit to Selma Jones (take report from school)*

Tuesday
9.30 *Meeting at Knightsbridge High School re planning for 5th year support group*
12.00 *Visit to Teri and Kevin Fowler*
PM: *in office – write up case notes re home visit and plans for Thursday's school group*

Wednesday
AM: On duty in office
2.00 Contact school re Kevin and arrange to visit Teri next week. Follow up the school information requested.
3.00 Home visit to Kerry Watson and her mum.
4.00 Home visit with guidance teacher to Sarah Knowles.

Thursday
9.30 (Group starts at 10am). Meet Karen at Knightsbridge School. Room 2514. (Take group work materials).
PM: On duty in office

Friday
10.00 Attendance at MAPPA meeting at Probation HQ. Take report on Shahida Fareem.
12.30 Lunch with Mary. Meet at Café Royale
2.30 Write report on Kerry Watson for next week's case conference.

Saturday

Sunday

Case Study 3.1

Aileen is a social worker in an educational social work service. She has received a referral about Kevin (aged 12) who has not been attending school regularly. When he has attended has presented as aggressive and unkempt.

Aileen meets Kevin and his mother Teri at their home to discuss how best she can support them and re-engage Kevin with his education. Teri and Kevin both appear very wary of Aileen, and Teri in particular says she hates social workers and does not want someone judging her. She has a negative view of previous involvement from the local mental health social work team, and has avoided contact with the service in recent months. Kevin is very quiet initially; it is clear that Aileen will need to spend time building up his trust. Teri states that she is feeling overwhelmed by events in her life and that she has tried everything to help Kevin but with no success.

Reflective Activity 3.1

1. What thoughts and feelings might impact on the way that Aileen communicates with Teri and Kevin?
2. Can you identify any personally held values and/or assumptions that you hold which may contribute to your impressions of the family?
3. What types of communication skills may be useful when trying to engage with Teri and Kevin? How might Teri and Kevin feel about Aileen?

Reflective Activity 3.1 will help the reader understand the actions and emotions of Aileen and others.

Communication and reflection: a starting point

The preceding chapters have highlighted the place of relationships in social work practice and the balance that this has in relation to professional roles. The location of relationships within a psycho-social sphere (Ruch, 2009) opens the door for considering all aspects of practice within a multi-faceted context (i.e. personal values, emotions, professional codes, organizational culture, socio-political context). Ward (2010) notes that this necessitates reflection and that we make sure that the context in which we communicate is as conducive as possible to informed and positive practice.These ideas are signposts to the core purpose of this book. Perhaps most crucial is the emphasis on the complex inter- and intra personal aspects of relationships. If we accept this complexity then reflection about the ways in which we communicate with service users, and about the drivers behind these approaches to communication, is seen to be crucial for understanding and refining practice. Ward (2010) stresses that communication in social work practice operates at an emotional and cognitive level. This is important when staking a claim for critical reflection, and elevates communication skills above the mere passing and receiving of information.

The model proposed in Chapter 1 highlights that these 'softer' (but still complex) features of social work practice need to be located alongside the 'harder' elements such as legislation, professional codes and theoretical knowledge. It is important to underline the relationship between the 'hard' and 'soft' features in order to make absolutely clear the central importance of communication skills. As noted in Chapter 1, Sudberry (2002) points out that without the establishment of a positive relationship the more tangible outcomes of practice will not emerge. Reynolds and Scott (1999) note that the establishment of a trusting and warm relationship requires a genuine human connection *before* service users will share their own perspectives, and that only then can these perpectives be tuned into, reflected back and explored in an empathic manner. It is quite clear that use of self and the potential of sharing one's own emotions may be crucial in both the establishment and maintenance stages of a positive relationship. It is not uncommon for social work students and practitioners to view communication skills as a given; as a universally held set of abilities. However, social work communication differs from informal social communication because of the underlying professional purpose, role and associated accountabilities (Lishman, 2009). Hennessey (2011) points out that empathic communication in social work must not be simply equated with friendship or unguarded personal disclosure, although it can also be argued that the desire for genuineness, trust, warmth and acceptance articulated within service user literature (Harding and Beresford, 1995) requires a degree of emotional involvement and exposure to establish a reciprocal relationship. These competing pressures will be present in any interaction in social work and justify the application of critical reflection about the skills we use, and why and how we use them. The guidance for social workers issued by the General Social Services Council (GSSC, 2011) in relation to professional boundaries emphasizes the word *professional* in the context of boundaries and the need for role and power to be reflected upon to avoid the potential negative impact on social workers of blurred boundaries. This chimes with the purpose of this book: evidently, social workers need to engage in reflection and ethical debates about their relationships with service users, and this reflection must then be *used* and communicated in the on-going practice of the social worker. It should be noted that this dynamic, reflective approach to managing professional boundaries intentionally sidesteps a list of rules to do with boundaries that can lead to unthinking and inflexible practice, instead recognizing that relationships are fluid and require constant reflection (GSSC, 2011).

Turning to the case study, Aileen will face many challenges when trying to communicate and engage with Teri and Kevin. Striking a balance between a professional role (underpinned by the legal requirement for Kevin to attend school) and the need to establish a positive working relationship with the family may present her with communication challenges. For example, if one considers the approach to questioning that Aileen may utilize in her first meeting, then the value of reflection will become evident. Open questions invite expansive responses and give a significant share of control to the service user in terms of the content of their answers (Koprowska, 2005). An example might be, 'Tell me about the difficulties you are having at school at the moment'. If Aileen were to put this style of question to Kevin at an early point in their first meeting she may find that he would find the potential broadness of the answer to the question intimidating and difficult to articulate. This could well be further exacerbated by a lack of trust at this stage in the relationship. In turn, Aileen may be irritated by the apparent lack of cooperation, and begin to feel that Kevin's presentation may be the root cause of his difficulties at school.

If Aileen engages in critical reflection, she may be able to see that her approach to the questioning was inhibiting Kevin, and that rather than giving power to Kevin to provide his own articulation of his situation, the question actually leaves him floundering and unsure how to respond. This level of reflection can then be deepened, and Aileen may recognize that her adoption of an open questioning approach was an attempt to 'get to the point' rather than focus on the establishment of a trusting relationship. There is a potential feedback loop in her approach to her communication, in that she may utilize a combination of open and closed questions to help engagement. Closed questions are more focused and tend to have a specific answer in mind (Lishman, 2009), for example 'What is your favourite subject at school?'. Kevin may find it easier to respond to this kind of question, and he is not required to expand upon his answers if he does not feel able. This could increase Kevin's confidence, and also impact on Aileen's feelings about him. The positive angle adopted in the closed question example above may also help to foster a relationship that is not characterized by implicit blame. Without the opportunity to engage in this simple example of reflection, it is possible to see how Aileen's approach to communication could be detrimental to both her relationship with Kevin and lead her to draw narrow impressions of his commitment and involvement. This hypothetical example may of course be turned on its head: the use of open questions might provide a liberating platform for Kevin to articulate his feelings and develop a keener understanding of his situation. What is crucial is that Aileen examines and reflects on these choices and on the impact that her experiences of communication have on her assessment of Kevin.

A framework for reflecting about communication

The concept of emotion was introduced in Chapter 1, and this gives us a good starting point for highlighting the importance of critical reflection in relation to the emotional content of relationships in social work. Ingram (2012b, 2013) noted that research findings on the cognitive appraisal aspects of emotions (Rosenberg, 1990; LeDoux, 1997) help social work to challenge the perceived incompatibility between emotions and informed practice. Ingram argues that the process of assigning a meaning to an emotional response triggers, by definition, a cognitive and reflective process in which the social worker must interpret what a presenting situation means and in turn respond and communicate appropriately. There is a great deal contained within the word *appropriately*, and it is here that this chapter may be of most use to the reader. The *appropriate* response will be constructed by the key aspects listed in Box 3.1.

The variables noted in Box 3.1 provide social workers with a framework for reflecting upon their communication skills. The key message is that social work communication is influenced by internal and external influences, and so critical reflection must engage

Box 3.1 A framework for reflection on communication in social work

- Personal values and experiences
- Professional codes, legislation and policy
- Role and purpose of interaction
- Nature of relationship between participants in an interaction
- Interpretation of verbal and non-verbal elements within the interaction
- Perceived expectations of appropriate behaviour within organizational culture

across these domains. Turner and Stets (2005, (p. 293)) sum up the importance of context when considering emotions:

> Emotions are the driving force behind the commitments to culture. Indeed emotions are what give cultural symbols the very meanings and power to regulate, direct, and channel human behaviour and to integrate patterns of social organization.

Simply put, they contend that emotions help individuals to prioritize, differentiate and understand the circumstances and stimuli they are involved with. These appraisals are also located within and influenced by the wider context of norms, culture and rules.

Returning to the case study, it is clear that Teri may well appear resistant and demoralized when first meeting with Aileen. Within the interaction both Teri and Aileen will be transmitting and interpreting the meaning of each other's communication. This is an important point, as it brings in the importance of Aileen considering her own presentation as well as making sense of what Teri may be communicating to her. This complex inter-personal exchange will contain both verbal and non-verbal elements. Trevithick (2005) notes the importance of considering the tone, pitch, volume and speed of the verbal elements of communication and the impact that these elements have on what is interpreted by the receiver. For example, Aileen may note that her own speech speeds up because of her anxiety about Teri's negative view of social work. Teri in turn may find Aileen's apparent rush as an indication that she does not have time to talk to her or that she is feeling anxious. These interpersonal judgments will be further informed by observation of non-verbal elements of communication (Sutton, 1979; Trevithick, 2005; Lishman, 2009). Non-verbal communication includes features such as facial expression, eye context, active listening and posture. These elements interact with the verbal elements and may reinforce or contradict what is being verbalized (Koprowska, 2005). For example, if Aileen's aforementioned rapid verbal delivery is coupled with lack of eye contact, Teri may well feel even more sure that Aileen is anxious and uncomfortable with her. However, if Aileen is able to maintain eye contact and a warm and friendly demeanour then this will go some way to off-set the information conveyed by the fast pace of her speech. The important point here is that Aileen must engage in reflection during the interaction *and* away from it to unpeel these layers to make sense of the efficacy of her communication and also increase her awareness of the impact of her communication practice on the development of a positive relationship with Teri and Kevin. Sutton (1979) draws a useful analogy of non-verbal elements of communication being like the instrumentation behind the words in a piece of music. The two simply exist intertwined with each other and both have an impact on the resultant meaning.

Personal values and emotional responses are key features of our communication framework. It is important to consider the impact of the immediate environment on communication. Ferguson (2010) vividly describes the impact of the sights, sounds and smells of practice. They affect the judgements we make as social workers, and in turn contribute to the way that we communicate. If the context of the interaction with Teri and Kevin was an interview room in a social work office, then the formality and associated professional power may appear more evident and in turn affect the meaning attached to what is communicated. For example, Aileen may find it more difficult to establish a trusting relationship with the family as the formality may feed into their preconceived negative expectations of the interaction. Alternatively, if the meeting took place in the family home, Aileen would be able to observe and process what additional meaning the home environment imparted to the interaction. For example, if the home was dark, unkempt and chaotic, this may reinforce Teri's expressed feelings of lack of control. The importance of this brief example is that the environment in which we communicate will impact on how we interpret what is being said and felt.

The framework in Box 3.1 also highlights what we have termed 'hard' features of the social work context. These include professional codes, polices, legislation and less concrete elements such as organizational culture. In some sense these provide a further contextual backdrop to any interaction, and in turn offer the social worker further food for thought when engaging in critical reflection. This brings in the *professional* role and the impact this has on the ways social workers communicate. Van Lanen (2008, p. 470) helpfully provides a definition of professionalism which allows space for social workers to consider their own actions:

> Professionalism... refers to the situation in which workers themselves are in possession of the specialised knowledge that is required for their work and are in possession of the discretionary power to organise their own conditions of work as opposed to being... subject to the will of... managers.

Part of the resistance that may be present in the relationship between Aileen and the family (to be picked up further in the next section of this chapter) may be related to the perceived power differential between the social worker and service user that comes with the statutory role and responsibility. In this case it will be tied up with the need for Kevin to be attending school, and the associated parental responsibilities that Teri has in this. This presents a vivid example of a point where Aileen must balance the 'harder' professional role with the 'softer' aspects of forming a positive relationship. Lishman (2009) notes the importance of explaining clearly to a service user the purpose of one's role. This links strongly with the notion of transparency and genuineness desired by service users (Harding and Beresford, 1995). It is crucial that Aileen is able to communicate her purpose in a way that makes clear to the family the nature of her involvement. This may help to ameliorate the initial lack of trust present and provide a strong foundation for on-going communication.

Organizational culture influences the ways that employees communicate and present themselves in practice (Hochschild, 1983). In the context of social work, Ingram (2012a) found that social workers felt that there was an implicit organizational message that required them to maintain an emotional distance from service users. This sits rather uncomfortably with the notion of genuine engagement associated with relationship-based practice (Hennessey, 2011). The implicit (or indeed explicit) organizational messages about the approach Aileen should adopt will have an impact on the way she chooses to communicate. It may be that there is a strong managerialist culture, in which case Aileen's prime accountability may be to the organization rather than the service user (Meagher and Parton, 2004). This puts pressure on Aileen to adopt a more formal and standardized approach to her practice,

> **Reflective Activity 3.2**
>
> Consider the framework in relation to a piece of practice you are involved with. List as many ideas as you can under each of the variables suggested.
>
> 1. Which aspects are useful to you and which aspects obstruct communication?
> 2. How can you use this information to inform future communication?

possibly at the expense of relationship formulation. As noted throughout this chapter, this may well undermine Aileen's ability to engage effectively with the family. Managerialist culture may display itself in terms of limited time allocated to cases in order to achieve targets and assessable outcomes. There may be many reasons for such an organizational backdrop; however it is crucial that social workers include this context in their framework for reflecting about communication.

Communication and working with resistance

One area of practice which can cause real anxiety for social workers is working with resistant service users. A theme of this book has been the importance of the relationship with the service user, but how does a social worker initiate a relationship with someone who does not want to be part of it? The required skills of engagement are central to social work practice and rely heavily on the ability to communicate. The temptation to engage in single-loop learning and to pursue a rational-technical course is heightened when the service user is hostile and unwilling to be engaged. It is all too easy in this circumstance to rationalize any difficulties or barriers as the 'fault' of the service user.

In relation to the case study, Aileen is likely to feel a range of emotions when faced with a hostile response from Teri. A flicker of fear (might she be aggressive or unpredictable?), anxiety about the task ahead, and especially about broaching the difficult subject of the care of Kevin, and a desire or instinct to 'escape.' Ferguson (2005) likens these emotions to the fear experienced by hostages held by captors, and points out that although social workers are not physically captured, they are held *in the relationship* by the requirements and demands of their jobs. Ferguson also notes that denial or repression of those emotions can lead to very poor practice whereby social workers do not consciously acknowledge the emotions, but act on them anyway. For example, Aileen might choose to view the situation as 'good enough' in order that she appease Teri and ingratiate herself (thus relieving the fear), and also so that she can leave the situation. Unconsciously driven by these emotional imperatives, Teri might look for positive evidence to back up her assessment that the situation is acceptable, and might play down or avoid uncovering evidence to the contrary. In other words, she might avoid asking the difficult questions.

Tallant, Sambrook and Green (2008), writing about dealing with offenders, state that initial engagement with potentially hostile service users can be summed up as follows: 'good engagement is about understanding that the starting point is discovering what the offender's view of their reality is' (p. 77). The authors suggest that this is not about condoning or agreeing with the service user, but is about seeking to fully *understand* their view of the situation. If Aileen is able to put this principle into action, for example, she might begin a discussion which facilitates Teri telling her about her past experiences with the mental health team and the way she views what went on. Aileen's job would not be to defend the agency, but rather to attempt to really understand how Teri felt about her experiences, by, for example, active listening and reflecting understanding back to Teri. A key aspect of the initial engagement process is the clear communication of the reasons why the social worker is there, and what their job involves. Trotter (2006) states that clarification of the role is of utmost importance, as without it, suspicion and mistrust may set in. Trotter (2006) and Ferguson (2005) also suggest that role clarification at the outset assists with the difficulty at the heart of many dealings with resistant or hostile service users: 'How do I ask the difficult questions?' Given that psychological processes are at play that give rise to the temptation or drive to self-preserving behaviour, how does a social worker resist that and continue to probe, whilst aware that intimidation or aggression might arise as a result? Both Trotter and Ferguson suggest that one resolution to this is for social workers to be very clear about the authoritative elements of their jobs. Ferguson states that 'much more openness is required about the authoritative role' in child protection, whilst Trotter suggests that workers with offenders should inform them of their statutory duties in reporting people to the Court, issuing warnings, informing the police etc. Ferguson also notes that social work education needs to recognize the potential dissonance between the Rogerian themes of unconditional positive regard and the circumstances in which social workers may feel very different types of emotions, and where they must articulate negative opinions, suspicion and disbelief.

So far then, it may be that Aileen is able to initiate engagement with Teri by making real efforts to understand how she views her situation. Aileen will be drawing on the communication skills covered throughout this chapter. She may also, at an appropriate juncture, explain her role in being able to help Teri with some of the things she may have spoken about, but also make it clear that she also has an unavoidable duty to ensure that Kevin 'is doing OK.' At this point, honesty about concerns is critical.

What might be going on, then, in terms of reflection? Emotionally, Aileen experiences the negative emotions described above, but needs to be able to *consciously* acknowledge that she is experiencing them. She may have an increased heart rate and other physiological symptoms which might lead her to act unthinkingly, unless she can reflect-in-action (Schon, 1983), understand what she is feeling and use her emotions productively. As Ingram (2013) states in relation to the emotional aspects of critical reflection, 'reflection... should feed back into actions rather than being an internal retrospective process' (p. 14). Therefore, Aileen might feel the negative emotions, reflect on them, reflexively think about the temptation to act in a self-preserving way, and thus be able to *avoid* unthinking 'flight' behaviour and, instead, channel her heightened feelings into real interest and active engagement in trying to understand Teri; knowing that this should de-escalate any potentially threatening situation.

After the initial engagement stage, Aileen might still feel as though she has a difficult task ahead. In further visits in response to problems, or after further concerns have been raised, how does she return to Teri's house to convey the unpleasant message that 'things are still not good enough?' The starting point for this stage in the relationship should be, according to Thompson (2009), the recognition of how the other person is feeling. Thompson suggests that sensitivity to this is essential, and that tentative phrases such as 'I can see that this is upsetting...' (p. 164) are helpful in that they can convey understanding without assuming knowledge of what is going on in the other person's mind. Thompson then suggests that moving things forward productively requires a move into a phase of negotiation. Negotiation should include separating the person

Reflective Activity 3.3

Think about a time when you felt fearful of a service user. Really try to recreate the situation and your emotional reaction (you could use role play or creative drama with colleagues).

1. Did you employ self-preservation techniques? What were they?
2. Did any of your strategies involve avoiding tackling the difficult issues? If so, how did you feel afterwards?

from the problem, and the generation of multiple solutions to the problem until one solution, acceptable to all parties, can be settled upon. Communication skills in this process are akin to skills of assertion, which can be summed up by differentiating them from aggression (bullying people) or passivity (allowing others to bully you) (Thomson, 2009). Thompson acknowledges that assertiveness requires a certain level of confidence, and thus, may be something that becomes easier with experience.

In terms of reflection and reflexivity, Aileen may explore whether she feels she is sufficiently assertive. Does she have the necessary confidence? If not, why not? In demonstrating sensitivity to Teri's feelings, what feelings of her own are running parallel? Is she frustrated that the situation has not improved? Does she feel uncomfortable about upsetting a fragile, but growing, relationship? Once again, the reflective process, and tuning into her own emotions, means that Aileen will not unthinkingly seek to avoid the difficult issues.

Chapter 1 explored the concept of 'disjuncture.' In this case, if Aileen were to slip into self-preservation behaviour and avoid asking the questions that she set out to ask, how might this make her feel in terms of value–behaviour congruence? It is likely she will feel uncomfortable and dissatisfied, knowing that she has not done her job properly. However, we have to ask whether this feeling should be classed as disjuncture, which is experienced when external, usually organizational, forces inhibit a worker from basing their practice on their values (Fenton, 2012)? In this case, *internal* mechanisms and processes have led to practice that is not based on the values of the profession, especially the values concerned with protecting people from harm. For example, the second ethical practice principle from the BASW Code of Ethics includes 'seeking to ensure that their (service users') behaviour does not harm themselves or other people' (BASW, 2012, p. 12). Aileen might feel that she has not done enough to protect Kevin, and thus her practice is at odds with her professional value base. Social workers anecdotally recount instances of driving away from situations and feeling very unhappy and uncomfortable because of the knowledge that they had not asked the difficult question or done their jobs as well as they should have. Might this be a form of *personal* or self-imposed disjuncture? Once again, this feeling can be an impetus for action in that if the social worker can reflect on the feeling and the reason why they are experiencing it, it may well lead to them taking remedial action by arranging to, for example, revisit the home. In this circumstance, renewed confidence and motivation for asking the questions might lead to proper planning and increased assertiveness.

Conclusion

This chapter has been firmly rooted in the model proposed in Chapter 1. It has been noted that the establishment of positive and effective relationships requires social workers to examine their personal values and their emotional responses to the situations and relationships in which they are involved. This requires an examination of the meanings and interpretations that they bring to bear on their practice. These will in part be informed by theory, legislation, policy and professional codes. However, they will also be very much rooted in the personally held constructs within each worker and the ways these impact on the way that they communicate.

In some ways, the purpose of this book is most acutely noticeable in the minutiae of interactions explored in this chapter. It is the complex network of variables and drivers at play in any given interaction which underline the inescapable importance of engaging in reflection, whether in the moment of practice or outwith it. Both types of reflection will be crucial in enabling social workers to understand how they communicate and the impact this may have on their practice, and will also help inform future practice.

Further resources

Lishman, J. (2009) *Communication in Social Work.*

Koprowska, J. (2005) *Communication and Interpersonal Skills in Social Work.*
Lishman (2009) and Koprowska (2005) provide a broad introduction to the key facets of social work communication.

Ruch, G., Turney, D. and Ward, A. (eds.) (2010) *Relationship-Based Social Work: Getting to the Heart of Practice.*
Covers the concept of relationship based practice thoroughly and in an applied manner.

CHAPTER 4

Undertaking life-changing assessments

Social workers undertake many different types of assessment, including assessment of need, risk assessment, parenting skills assessment, and assessments of financial circumstances. This chapter will consider how reflection can enhance and enable effective assessment processes and outcomes, by considering the following:

- Assessment and influencing factors
- Understanding the role of reflection in assessment
- Emotions and assessment
- Power, empowerment and the value base of assessment.

Steve's diary (Hospital Social Worker)

Monday
9.30 _Team meeting (x 4 cases)_
1.30 _Read Maria's notes/prepare for meeting_
(*_reminder – check discharge notes_)
2.30 _Meet with Maria – Ward 10_
3.45 _Meet with Andrew – Ward 6_

Tuesday
Catch Dr Scott & phone Maria's husband for appointment.
10.30 _meet with Dot – Ward 7_
Make appointment with Dot's family
2.00 _Susan and Philip – Ward 5_

Wednesday
9.30 Ward 7
11.00 meet with Dot's family
12.30 Lunch with team
2.15 Ward 6
3:30 Write notes for Support and Supervision
4.30 Meet with Maria's husband

Thursday
10.00 Support and Supervision (Main Building)
(Note* Discuss dealing with differences in
opinion of the case and family)
2.00 Reflection (Room 1.7 McKenzie)
3.00 Ward 7

Friday
10.00 Reflection on cases
11.30 Dot's Report
12:45 Meet with Andrew
2.00 Elsie's Report
3.30 Meet with Dr Murphy and staff nurse

Saturday

Sunday

Case Study 4.1

Steve has been qualified for a year and is a social worker in a
hospital team. He is required to work across several wards and has
responsibility for ensuring the safe discharge of patients. There is

always considerable pressure to get patients out of hospital quickly in order to ensure those who can be discharged do not remain in hospital unnecessarily. Working with different age groups and people who have different medical conditions requires Steve to work closely with medical colleagues at all times.

One of the patients Steve is currently assessing is Maria who is 42 and diagnosed with oesophageal cancer. Maria has undergone radiotherapy, chemotherapy and surgery but her prognosis is terminal. She has become increasingly ill over the past few weeks resulting in numerous admissions to hospital. Maria has expressed a wish to be at home to die but her husband, Paul, is extremely anxious about this and would much rather Maria remained in hospital or was discharged to a hospice. Paul and Maria have two sons aged 9 and 12, and Paul is worried about how they are coping. He and Maria disagree on how to talk to them about their mother's death.

Another of the cases Steve is working with is Dot, who is 94 and fiercely independent. Dot had a nasty fall and her family now feel it is time she moved from her home into residential care. Dot agrees her home is now too much for her to manage, but is not sure about moving into a residential setting because she is worried about losing her independence.

Steve must complete assessments for Maria and Dot as part of the discharge and multi-agency support plans.

Starting an assessment means starting out on a process which should gather together information already known and seek to ascertain new information relevant to what or who is being assessed. Social workers are often assessing very difficult and upsetting situations, and so need to be prepared for the impact the assessment may have on others as well as on themselves.

Reflective Activity 4.1

1. What factors make Steve's assessment of Maria and Dot difficult?
2. What issues of power and empowerment might Steve need to consider when undertaking his assessment of Maria and Dot?
3. How might Steve be affected by these assessments?
4. Where do you think Steve might find support to help him with reflection on the assessment?
5. How might Steve's assessment impact on other members of the multi-agency discharge and support team?
6. What would you do in Steve's position? Why is that?

Reflective Activity 4.2

Have a look at your diary for the next week and build in some reflective space where you can consider the above questions in relation to your own assessment activity.

What models and techniques might you use to assist with your reflections about such issues (see Chapter 2)? Why? Later reflect on how effective they were.

During a typical week Steve, like all other social workers, needs to manage his diary to ensure he has time to complete his assessments within the deadlines set by his organization and by his service users. At times this can be difficult, as pressures may compete, for example there are always demands to manage resources efficiently which in turn results in pressure to ensure timely discharge from hospital and avoid any delay. However, some patients need more time spending with them in order to gather appropriate information for the assessment and to support them through the assessment and discharge process. It is important that in managing his diary he also ensures time is set aside for thinking and reflecting upon an assessment, as this reflective process can assist his understanding of individuals' circumstances as well as help him understand where pressures exist and how they might impact on the assessment process and outcomes.

Assessment and influencing factors

Assessment is both an inherent and an explicit aspect of social work practice, which has evolved as social work as a profession has evolved. Historically, services introduced during Victorian times to ensure the health and education of children developed as more dedicated services, such as social work, emerged to ensure standards in childcare were maintained (Ferguson, 2004; Webb, 2007; Hodson, 2011). Inherent within the process of ensuring children are educated, healthy and cared for appropriately are processes of assessment that seek to measure one child's progress against another in the context of socially constructed and legally defined frameworks.

Whilst assessment might be regarded as always having been an inherent social work task, as an explicit process it has a much shorter history. Gray (2002) pinpoints the Children Act 1948 as a period when the term 'assessment' became part of the statutory language, although only then in relation to children in the care system. In 1981, following a wide-ranging review of assessment by a government working party, the following definition of assessment was offered:

A continuous process whereby problems are identified and appropriate responses decided upon. (Department of Health and Social Security, 1981, cited in Gray, 2002, p. 170.)

The concept of a continuous process is very relevant to reflective assessment practice because it is important to recognize that practice does not stand still in time. Individual practitioners develop their assessment skills as they reflect upon each assessment they undertake and also as part of the reflective process that occurs in other activities such as supervision, peer support, reading and report writing. In recent years, moves to standardize processes have impacted significantly on social work practice and as a consequence there has been concern that social workers have become caught up in the managerial aspects of assessment. Child protection social work in England perhaps most notably highlights the ways in which managerial approaches can compromise social workers' skills and result in assessments which do not embody reflective approaches and analysis.

The inquiry by Lord Laming following the death of Victoria Climbié on 25 February 2000 emphasized systemic failures across agencies responsible for protecting children and called for greater accountability of agencies, a strengthening of inter-agency recording procedures and increased management of front-line professionals (Cm 5730, 2003 and Corby, 2006). The Integrated Children System (ICS) was designed to provide an electronic record of professional involvement, assessment, decision making and review from first point of contact to case closure in order to ensure children could not fall through the safety net of professional involvement (Cleaver et al., 2008). Becoming operational in LAs in Wales on 31 December 2006 and in LAs in England on 1 January 2007, the system embodied the principles of information-sharing central to good assessment practice. However, Broadhurst et al. (2009) looked at social work initial assessment undertaken using the *Assessment Framework* (DoH, 2000) and found performance management and the ICS prompted workers to gather information in a systematic way. They also found the computerized systems meant the imposed drive to maintain workflow suppressed the basic principle of supporting families, particularly so in busy teams. Research has highlighted that prescriptive approaches to assessment actually create the potential for error, as social workers spent time trying to work around and manage computer systems rather than using their professional skills to work with families (Broadhurst et al., 2008; Horwath, 2011). Similarly, the Munro report (2011) identified that social workers' engagement skills and working alongside the most vulnerable people in society had been compromised by managerial procedures. Significantly the Munro report highlighted the importance of professionals developing their knowledge and capabilities in order to ensure skill in intervention, critical reflection and analysis. Likewise, Horwath (2011) identified that challenging and changing managerial systems was only part of the issue, and that social workers needed to have the right workloads and access to supervision and training if organizational cultures were to change.

Whilst the experience of child protection social work in England highlights the issue of managerialism, this is not a scenario unique to England or to child protection work. Back in 1999 Goddard and colleagues found that in Australia a drive towards standardized assessment tools designed to reduce risk actually served to increase the danger of poor assessment because the form-filling became routine. Moreover, skill and professional discretion gave way to reliance on categorizing similarities in behaviour as opposed to understanding an individual family and its circumstances (Goddard, Saunders and Stanley, 1999). Crisp et al. (2007) compared four different assessment frameworks designed for use with different service user groups of children, drug users, older people and carers, and found that implicit within the frameworks was an assumption that the assessors were skilled and able to articulate their reasoning and actions. However, if used by inexperienced practitioners or used as a mechanistic checklist, the assessment tool's potential to contribute to effective practice was significantly limited, and so the need for training and supervisory support was important.

In some spheres of practice, particularly in the statutory sector, there is also potential to assume that the completion of assessment documentation is always a requirement before a service can be provided. As Beckett (2010) highlights, agencies often have elaborate assessment procedures which may involve many sets of complicated documents and the input of data into online formats and this process may become, incorrectly, regarded as 'the assessment'. It is important to remember that the completion of paperwork, forms and inputting data is not the actual assessment, it is the official and important record of what has been found and analysed during a process of assessment. The actual assessment is the formation of a professional judgement which occurs in the engagement with service users, and in the formal and informal reflective discussions with colleagues and supervisors.

Assessment tools are helpful and, as identified by Horwath (2011), can impose much-needed structure on assessments, particularly for inexperienced social work practitioners. However, as identified above, it is important to recognize that the assessment tool is only one aspect of a very complex process which relies heavily on the skills of the social worker in planning the assessment, gathering information, analysing information and ultimately in presenting findings in a coherent written format (see Chapter 8). Deconstructing the process of assessment highlights its complexity and in turn highlights the range of skills social workers need in order to become competent assessors. In order to be a skilled assessor, social workers must be skilled communicators (in both verbal and written form), and able to interpret and analyse a wide range of information such as child growth charts, psychiatric reports, legal and procedural documents and case files. Social workers need to be able to recognize the complexity of people's lives and understand how issues of social justice, access to community resources and government policy all impact on an individual's well-being. Above all, social workers need to be able to elicit information from the individuals and families they work with, not all of whom will want to volunteer information readily.

To achieve high standards in assessment, social workers need to have the emotional intelligence to adapt their approach and style to the presentation of individual service users and their families, always aiming to ensure maximum engagement in the assessment process. Throughout the assessment, social workers must be respectfully critical of information shared with them by service users and by other professionals or members of the public, and be mindful of the legal and procedural context within which they practice. Finally, social workers must recognize that when they are asked to complete an assessment they are not being asked to tick meaningless boxes on a form and 'wedge' information they have about individuals into pre-existing preforms. What they are being asked to do is arrive at a coherent professional judgement based on the information available to them – a professional judgement based on reflective analysis of complex information and recorded in an accurate and systematic way.

Understanding the role of reflection in assessment

Assessment often takes up a significant proportion of social workers' time, regardless of the practice setting or service user group. It is, therefore, important that social workers understand the purpose of assessment as well as the process and potential outcomes, and that they become skilled in using assessment tools and models to support their professional judgements. Reflective practice is integral to assessment both in terms of ensuring effective and appropriate use of tools and models and in developing the analysis of information gathered during assessment. Additionally, using reflection in assessment will militate against oppressive assessment processes which do not consider the needs of the person being assessed and their family.

The title of this chapter refers to 'life-changing assessments', which may at first sight imply looking only at the more overtly serious aspects of social work practice. It is the case that some assessments have obvious 'life-changing' implications, for example child protection investigations may lead to children being removed from the care of their family; in Scotland, social work assessments to inform sentencing in criminal proceedings may result in a person being detained in prison; and assessments as to the likelihood of someone posing a risk to themselves or others in mental health cases may contribute to admission to hospital and imposition of treatment. Consider the case studies above; if Steve's assessment of the discharge plan for Maria is that she should be taken home to die then this will have a significant impact on the lives of her husband and children. Discharge from hospital may indeed be the outcome Maria wants from the assessment but the consequences may be life-changing by virtue of affecting the way that a significant loss in the life of the family will occur. Likewise, an assessment that leads to Dot moving into residential care may make her physically safe but will have huge emotional consequences which she may find difficult to adjust to. In short, all social work assessments form part of the much larger picture of people's lives and as such may have life-changing consequences. The consequences may not be immediately obvious or significant enough to seem to warrant

Reflective Activity 4.3

Consider an assessment you had responsibility for completing or being part of.

1. Why was this assessment necessary?
2. Why was it important to think about how the information might be gathered for the assessment?
3. What impact did the feelings of those being assessed have on the assessment?
4. How did your feelings impact on the assessment?
5. Did you include any reflections in the recording of the assessment?
6. How might your reflection on this assessment help you with future assessments?
7. How might broader stereotypic perceptions about elderly or terminally ill people impact your view on the case?

thorough reflection but, none the less, an understanding of what is informing the decision-making process for the social worker (values, professional code, life experiences, previous professional decisions or emotions) is always important.

Emotions and assessment

Looking at the case studies it can be seen that Steve's assessments will be complex. For example, for Maria, who is terminally ill and wishes to die at home, he needs to assess both the practicalities of palliative care in the home and the enormous emotional impact on Maria, her husband and two sons. Steve's assessment must support him and other professionals in arriving at an appropriate discharge plan, but from the outset he will need to balance Maria's wishes and feelings against those of her husband, Paul, who will undoubtedly be her primary carer if she returns home. This may also require Steve to complete a separate assessment of Paul in his own right as a carer.

Emotional intelligence requires social workers to have insight into their own feelings and to understand how they then impact on others. Ingram (2013) argues that emotionally intelligent social workers are more adequately equipped to develop and sustain relationships. In Maria's case it is likely that Steve will need to consider his own feelings about death and dying, and possibly even reflect on how he has coped with the death of people close to him. Additionally, he will be tuning into the emotional world of Paul, and will need to consider the drivers and emotional cues behind Paul's standpoint and manage these in conjunction with his assessment of Maria. This emotionally intelligent conception of the process drives Steve necessarily into the arena of reflection and reflexivity. It requires him to bring his self-knowledge to bear within a wider context of resources, legislation and service user perspectives. Given the emotional nature of the assessment, Steve would probably need to discuss the assessment in supervision and might also want to engage in informal discussion with his work colleagues. As discussed in Chapter 9, supervision is a tool or resource to enable professional reflection and is central to developing skills and knowledge. It is also a means of enabling social workers to understand how their values may impact on their work, in this case, how Steve's values may impact on his assessment of Maria. As suggested in Chapter 2, he might benefit from having a critical friend with whom he can discuss his emotions whilst maintaining the confidentiality of the service users.

Beckett (2010) pointed out that undertaking an assessment requires intrusion into people's personal lives and may sometimes prompt social workers to question whether their involvement is having a positive or negative impact. Questioning the purpose of assessment is the first step in identifying whether, indeed, an assessment is required, and if it is, who and what is the focus of the assessment. Lack of consideration of these factors in the planning phase can lead to time and resources being wasted and service users being subject to inappropriate intrusion into their lives, the outcome of which is undoubtedly oppressive practice.

Dominelli (2009) identified that anti-oppressive practice is a complex notion encompassing issues of social justice, human rights and ever-evolving social and political ideologies. As such, acting anti-oppressively requires social workers to understand their own value base and emotions and reflect on how they impact on practice. In busy teams, where social workers are managing competing demands and complex case loads, questioning the purpose, scope and approach to assessment is central to effective time and resource management. Equally, developing an understanding of the emotional (and sometimes emotive) issues faced on a day-to-day basis, and reflecting on how this may impact on the assessment, can enhance anti-oppressive practice. It is not unusual in social work to be faced with distressing information. For example, listening to a child's disclosure of abuse, working with a convicted sexual offender to assess risk, or responding to angry or verbally abusive people will inevitably have an emotional impact on the social worker and subsequently may influence the assessment. The use of reflective practice in assessment can, therefore identify where the social worker's emotions and emotional responses might be impacting on their professional judgements and also highlight adherence to the principles of anti-oppressive practice.

Power, empowerment and the value base of assessment

Inherent in assessment is a complex power imbalance between the assessor, as someone who gathers information and who also often holds the metaphorical key to accessing or rationing resources, and the assessed, who is being judged against whatever criteria are being applied. Quite often there is also the need to balance issues of empowerment with the social control aspects of practice, for example whilst a child protection assessment might be needed to ensure a child's safety it is likely to feel like a negative and disempowering experience for some, if not all, members of the child's family.

Not only is there a complex power imbalance but also a requirement for the assessor to understand the impact of assessment on the decision-making process, planning and resources allocation as well as the complex array of law, policy and procedures (Milner and O'Byrne, 2009) . As identified in Chapter 1, law, policy and procedure, the 'hard' features of practice, are guiding features of what social workers are required to do, and assessment practice highlights this clearly. Earlier in this chapter, discussion showed how assessment practice reduced to form filling might limit the opportunity for social workers to use their important core skills in relation to engagement with vulnerable people. The softer skills associated with social work are key here to ensure the assessment process is one which adheres to the legal and procedural context of the assessment but which is moulded to reflect the individual circumstances and needs being assessed.

The balance between social work values and the recognition of the complex individual, organizational and legislative context may give rise to a sense of disjuncture for social workers (Fenton, 2012;

see also Chapter 6). Simply put, the values of a worker may be at odds with the imperatives of the wider drivers behind an assessment. This requires social workers to be able to critically reflect upon factors which influence daily work and may have an impact on an assessment, such as pressure to vacate hospital beds, timescales for court hearing and child protection conferences or statutory review periods for care plans. In turn, social workers must be able to manage the ethical stress inherent in such circumstances, ethical stress which arises from recognition of the rationale for the influencing factors set against the actual impact the influencing factors may have on the individual service user. Social workers are required, therefore, to seek ways to navigate a way through the assessment that reduce the disjuncture and seek to maintain an approach focused on the service user. Such tensions are familiar in social work discourse, but to leave them unexplored within an assessment process may lead to oppressive practice.

There are many complex issues social workers must face when completing an assessment, not least of which is identifying who actually is the service user central to the assessment. Hodson (2011) looks at pre-birth assessment and argues that child protection procedures are focused on the unborn child, who has no legal rights, and so potentially ignore the rights of the pregnant woman. The case studies above also highlight the complex issues social workers can face in assessment. Although Maria is defined as the 'service user', the needs of her husband and her children are of equal importance to the practical and emotional needs of Maria. Likewise, when assessing Dot's needs and wish to return to her own home Steve must not only take account of the practicalities of where Dot will live but the huge emotional impact the change will have on her or those close to her. In order to complete his assessments Steve will need to discuss difficult issues, not least of which relate to the family's views and fears, taking into account the wishes and feelings of the service user and dealing with how they may conflict with the views of their families. Supporting Maria to experience the end-of-life care she most wants will require Steve to support other members of the family in accepting her wishes. Equally, working with Dot to identify what support she wants and enable her to review options for community care and residential care will undoubtedly require Dot and her family to consider the physical and emotional risks she will face with each option.

Reflecting on personal and professional values and their impact on the assessment process is important, as the social worker's values may directly conflict with the values of the service users and their family values. For example, Steve's own values relating to end-of-life care and his personal experience of death will impact on his understanding of how Maria and her family are feeling. Christ and Sormanti (2000) highlight that knowledge and theory of death and dying are often not integrated into practice, in part owing to lack of training, and so it is reasonable to assume Steve will be drawing primarily on his personal experiences. Likewise, his experience of ageing and the experiences of members of his own family getting older will shape how he feels about Dot and what is the most appropriate discharge plan for her. However, the assessment is not about Steve's views, although he will need to convey a professional judgement that will inevitably be influenced by his personal values and experience as well as his academic knowledge and practice experience. The purpose of the assessment is to inform a specific and individual discharge plan, and, as noted above, stage one of the reflective process is to identify and understand the actual purpose of the assessment. The next stage is understanding how the social worker shapes and impacts upon the assessment.

As identified in Chapter 2, in a culture of reflection, social workers can develop an understanding of their beliefs, assumptions and feelings relating to practice. Most importantly social workers need to understand how their values will impact on the fundamental element of engaging with the person who is being assessed. Morrison (2007), writing about emotional intelligence and emotional social work, commented:

> Whilst assessment is commonly described as the first stage of the care or intervention process, in fact, assessment cannot be effective unless there has first been attention to a process of engagement and rapport building with the service user (Morrison, 2007, p. 235).

Often in social work practice it is necessary to assess people who hold very different opinions and beliefs to the assessor, and the potential barriers this creates must be recognized and addressed. For example, assessing the long-term placement options for a child in care may require social workers to consider harrowing information about the particular child's experiences. Issues such as physical or sexual abuse of children or adults are not issues in the sphere of most people's experience, but for social workers they are something they frequently have to deal with. As a consequence, the ability to assess those who have experienced abuse as well as those who have perpetrated it is essential. Having the skill to do this well requires significantly more than an ability to follow a pre-defined assessment tool, and reflective practice supports the process of arriving at a defensible professional judgement. The use of reflective tools and models, such as those identified in Chapter 2, can be of great value: prompting social workers to stop and think about what is actually enabling or preventing engagement with people and how this may consequently impact on the assessment process as a whole.

Reflecting on the power imbalances and the value base within an assessment and the ultimate impact on the service user requires discussion with peers, both informally and formally, and in supervision. This is not to suggest that each assessment needs supervisory discussion but that critical reflection of one's own value base is something which should form part of on-going professional development. Individual reflection and reflexivity are important as a starting point but, as highlighted in Chapter 9, supervision provides the opportunity to critically reflect on practical issues relating to case work and to identify personal values and the ways that they may or may not impact on practice. Supervision can also be a space where the impacts of others, including the service user, family members and other professionals, can be discussed and analysed in relation to how they may shape or influence (both positively and negatively) the assessment process. Steve, for example, will need to understand his own emotional strengths and vulnerabilities and how they will affect his talking with service users and their families about their feelings, expectations and anxiety surrounding discharge. Supervisory discussion will also enable Steve to prepare for difficult discussions about the content of the assessment and also deepen his understanding of the ways that his values may affect such discussion.

Analysing and completing an assessment

Whilst assessment can be identified as a continuous process it is not one without an end: deadlines are a feature of social work practice – and for good reason. As Chapter 5 shows, assessment is not something which is totally separate and distinct from intervention, therefore a clear understanding of the purpose and time-scale of involvement is important. People's right to privacy is enshrined in human rights law and although some assessments carry a statutory requirement to assess even the most private of issues there is no mandate for endless intrusion. Good analysis is crucial to effective time-limited assessment, and recognition of and adherence to deadlines must not be ignored.

Understanding the end point or deadline for an assessment should really be the starting point for planning. Looking at Steve's diary it is clear he has many other tasks to complete during his working week and it is not unusual in social work to be juggling many competing pressures. Good time management is therefore essential, and creating time in the diary to allow for assessment analysis and the writing up of the assessment document is a key to success. Steve needs to understand the hospital discharge policy, work alongside other colleagues such as nurses, oncologists, geriatricians, and occupational therapists, have links with community resources and possibly liaise with social work colleagues in community teams who may be taking over case responsibility post-discharge. Simply contacting all of these people takes time, but on top of that Steve needs to incorporate the information they share into his assessment and analyse the impact the information has on the discharge plan. Steve's assessment is likely to be a powerful tool in the discharge process, and as such it is important for him to reflect on an infinitely large number of variable factors in order to ensure the assessment is a means of empowerment for his service users and a clear and transparent record of his professional practice for the agency and the family concerned (see Chapter 8).

Analysis can be something which occurs as a result of informal discussion with other members of the team or other professionals involved in the case as well as with the service user and their family. Analysis may also be something which occurs as the social worker personally reflects upon the information available to them. Time for reflection is crucial in this analysis, so that all perspectives are taken into account, and as Fook and Gardner (2007) highlight, it is important that the assessment aligns with the social worker's own professional moral code. In Steve's case, pressure from the family and the hospital to make a quick decision may mean that Steve misses out this reflective process of considering how his own value base and experiences might be influencing the assessment.

Time must be allocated to allow an assessment to be written: the importance of this cannot be overstated. The writing of an assessment requires the social worker to process a large volume of

Reflective Activity 4.4

Consider an assessment you are involved in.

1. Why is it important that cognizance is given to the language in an assessment?
2. Consider time factors – what part do they play in assessment?
3. If you had similar issues, whom could you discuss these with?

information into a particular document which will inform a decision-making process. This will require a high degree of skill in actually presenting written information succinctly, accurately and professionally, as assessments are often read by other professionals. However, it is also important to remember assessments are usually about a particular service user and their family, and they are the primary audience; so a great deal of skill is required in the way that information is presented accurately, clearly and sensitively (see Chapter 8). The use of language is highly significant, and understanding how the service user feels about what is written is important. In the case examples, Maria and Dot are aware of their circumstances but seeing something in writing can be more traumatic than hearing comments. Steve will need to write about Maria's prognosis and her wishes about where she wants to die. Similarly, he will need to talk about Dot's age and the impact of ageing on her independence. However, he will also need to reflect upon how the written word will impact on Maria's and Dot's feelings and the feelings of their respective families.

Conclusion

Chapter 1 highlighted how social work practice in any setting is contextualized by certain key, 'hard' features such as legislation, policy, procedure and theory. When considering assessment the 'hard' features may also include the assessment models, tools and even prescriptive forms and paperwork. It is essential for social workers to understand and have the relevant knowledge to underpin their practice and inform their use of the 'hard' features of assessment. It is, however, vital for social workers to be able to move beyond the structural framework surrounding assessment and develop the softer skills and engage with the circumstances surrounding each service user.

Models of reflection identified in Chapter 2 are extremely helpful in developing reflective practice in assessment, and can support both the process of information gathering as well as analysing information. As can be seen from the Reflective Social Work Practitioner Model (Figure 1.1), the social worker must consider a significant number of different and sometimes competing factors. When undertaking assessment this will require a critically analytical approach to incidents and emotions affecting the service user, their family and sometimes even other professionals all of which might impact on information shared in an assessment. In analysing this information the social worker must also be aware of their own value base and be willing to deconstruct and challenge inherent power dynamics, which is an important aspect of critical reflection (Chapter 2).

In the case study, Steve was faced with structural features such as hospital discharge time-scales and access to the finite resources needed to support Maria and Dot in their own home. Whilst he may have felt constrained by these factors, Steve also needed to ensure they did not prevent Maria and Dot achieving the outcomes they wished, namely to return to their own home with an appropriate support package. Had Steve employed single-loop thinking, as discussed in Chapter 2 (Figure 2.1), it is possible he may have approached the assessment from a rational-technical perspective and as such concluded that Maria would best receive the necessary medical care if she was discharged from hospital to a hospice and Dot would be safer in residential care. This approach may not have reflected the actual feelings, values and emotions expressed by Maria and her family or Dot and her family but might have been appealing options from a case load management perspective.

Using double-loop reflection (Figure 2.2), Steve listened to what each individual family member said but most importantly listened to what Maria and Dot said about what they wanted to happen. This approach required Steve to listen to some difficult information, particularly in relation to loss, bereavement, fear and anxiety, and in order to do this he needed to be aware of his own feelings and responses. However, by re-assessing and evaluating different perspectives Steve was able to use the assessment process reflectively, to shape what happens and to ensure the families had an outcome from the assessment which was appropriate for their needs.

Further resources

Parker, J. and Bradley, G. (2010) *Social Work Practice: Assessment Planning and Review.*
Provides an overview aimed at student social workers to enable skill development for practice and, as such, focus on the general 'how to' aspects of assessment.

Beckett, C. (2010) *Assessment and Intervention in Social Work, Preparing for Practice.*
An excellent text, aimed at student social workers and using case studies to highlight some key issues such as assessing need, judgement and risk.

Milner, J. and O'Byrne, P. (2009) *Assessment in Social Work,* 3rd Edition.
Reviews key issues linked to social work assessment. It also analyses concepts of power and anti-oppressive practice in relation to effective assessment practice.

Thompson, S. and Thompson, N. (2008) *The Critically Reflective Practitioner.*
An overview of reflective approaches relevant to the inclusion of reflection in assessment.

CHAPTER 5

Critically informed interventions

This chapter will build on the previous chapter on assessment and look at social work intervention. In order to begin to understand social work intervention and the role of reflective practice, this chapter will cover the following themes:

- The linking and differentiating between assessment and intervention
- Identifying the beginning and end of intervention and the influence of 'hard' and 'soft' features
- Intervention and anti-oppressive practice
- Applying the reflective practitioner models to intervention.

Tracy's Diary (Adult, Community-Based Team Social Worker)

Monday
9.30 *Admin tasks: Read referral from hospital about Dot and Steve's assessment Read case notes on newly allocated cases*
12.00 *Phone Steve at Hospital. Leave message for him.*
3pm *Early finish (Time off in lieu)*

Tuesday
10.00 *Visit to Dot and family at home.*
11.30 *Try to phone Steve*
12.00 *Support and supervision (note* no contact from the hospital social worker)*
3.00 *Write case notes and reports*

Wednesday
10.00 Visit to Helen Standing at home
11.30 Write up case notes
2.00 Visit to Alan Bell at home
2.45 Phone home help administrator.

Thursday
10.00 Team Meeting
12.00 Return call from Steve about Dot &
phone Dot's daughter
1.30 Meet new social work student!

Friday
10 Reflections and thoughts about Dot's case
3.00 Visit to Dot and Family

Saturday

Sunday

Case Study 5.1

The hospital social worker, Steve, completed assessments relating to the discharge plans for Maria, a patient terminally ill with oesophageal cancer, and Dot, a very independent 94-year-old admitted to hospital following a fall. Steve's assessment of Maria identified a support package to enable her to leave hospital to die at home with her family. Although Maria's case is complex, and the assessment raised many emotional issues for Steve, from an intervention perspective there was limited requirement for his social work skills at the point of discharge as the necessary expertise lay with the palliative care specialists. Beyond the discharge-planning meeting Steve's only intervention was to pass relevant information gathered in his assessment to the palliative care team.

Dot, on the other hand, required much more social work intervention. Steve's assessment identified Dot needed daily support at home provided by care staff every morning and evening. In addition, Dot's three daughters would call in during the day to help with meals and generally checking on how she was coping. Following the discharge-planning meeting the case transferred to the adult, community-based social work team.

The community-based social worker, Tracy, was allocated Dot's case. Unfortunately, due to staffing difficulties, Tracy had not been allocated the case until after the discharge meeting so, in preparation for her first visit to Dot, Tracy had read through Steve's assessment and tried to phone him to gather any additional information not been captured in the written assessment. However, due to the busy nature of social work, Tracy and Steve had not managed to talk to each other prior to Tracy visiting Dot and her family.

The assessment indicated that Tracy's primary intervention was care management, focusing on keeping the care package running smoothly, reviewing the care plan within statutory time-scales and making amendments if circumstances changed. However, at the first home visit it was evident Dot's daughters were extremely anxious, fearing their mother might fall again and seriously hurt herself. They felt strongly that Dot would be safer in residential care and that Steve's assessment was totally wrong and ill informed. Dot was very clear that she wished to end her days in her own home where she had lived for the last 74 years. She explained that one of the doctors had told her 'it was time to go into a home where she could be looked after properly' but that Steve had been really helpful; he spent time talking to her about her options and he had explained she could stay at home with support. Dot said she was so pleased Steve had recognized that. Whilst she was afraid of having another fall, living out her life in her own home, no matter what the consequences or risks, was what she wanted. Tracy reflected upon the content of Steve's assessment and recognized her intervention would also require more direct social work input around mediation in order to ensure Dot's wishes and hopes were not ignored.

Reflective Activity 5.1

1. If you were Tracy, what emotional issues might Dot and her daughters be facing that that you would need to think about in preparation for future discussions?
2. What are some of the professional tensions here is terms of conflicting professional values?
3. What risks might Dot be taking and how might issues of risk impact on your interventions? (see also Chapter 6)
4. Do you feel the daughters have a valid concern about their mother? If so, how would you feel about potentially attempting to help change Dot's perspective? What are the ethical concerns and power issues associated with trying to change Dot's perspective?

As identified in Chapter 1, the context of social work practice requires a balance between technical knowledge and the relationships-based aspects of the work. Social workers must understand and make appropriate use of both the 'hard' and 'soft' features relevant to each situation. In order to understand what is and is not 'appropriate' it is essential to reflect upon factors which will inevitably shape the intervention offered or provided.

Linking and differentiating assessment and intervention

Assessment and intervention are inextricably linked, and in some instances may even be the same thing. However, the extent to which they overlap or are distinct will depend very much on the practice setting. Some social work teams are more focused on short-term pieces of work primarily linked to formulating an assessment of what needs to happen next, whilst others may have long and very involved intervention with people over many months if not years. In the case study above, for example, Steve is primarily focused on assessment and discharge planning, working with very short time-scales linked to medical need and discharge policy and procedure. Conversely, in teams such as Looked After Children's Teams, Mental Health Teams, Disability Teams and, as for Tracy in the case study, Adult, Community-Based Teams, agency procedures are likely to direct social workers toward long-term relationship building, with the service user primarily focused on intervention and assessment being more a matter of updating and reviewing existing information.

When it comes to arriving at a definition of intervention it becomes clear that the overlap between assessment and intervention is often indistinct and interchangeable. In Chapter 4 it was noted that assessment is a complex and on-going process often surrounded by elaborate procedures and paperwork. However, the paperwork is not the assessment. The assessment is something which occurs in the engagement with service users and involves the process of gathering and analysing complex information from a range of sources: it is a professional judgement. Therefore, it relies heavily on the social worker's professional and interpersonal skills; in this respect assessment is the same as intervention. Beckett (2010, p. 44), suggests that 'quite often assessment is the easy bit. Recognizing the problems that need addressing and even getting a sense of what is causing those problems, though challenging in itself, is very often a relatively straightforward task as compared to deciding what to actually do'. This is not to suggest that assessment is only about gathering information, as the analysis is extremely important. However, it does highlight the more contained nature of assessment as a distinct task often with a clear start and end-point, which is what does often differentiate it from intervention.

Horner (2009) remarks that intervention is what the social work profession is about because it is a practical profession requiring so much more than theoretical observation and analysis. Intervention is, therefore, defined as doing something, delivering services, carrying out tasks and attempting to improve or control situations. Wilson et al. (2011) suggest that any case a social worker will encounter can be thought of and broken down into a series of steps or stages each of which will require issues addressing or questions to be answered. This is perhaps a helpful way of thinking about intervention, particularly in relation to reflection, as each individual step or stage may prompt different feelings and emotions. Beckett (2010) stresses that intervention occurs each time a social worker impacts on the life and environment of the families they work with, and that this also includes taking action even when someone does not actually want or welcome the intervention. However, intervention is not something which should be thought of simply in relation to social workers impacting on an individual. Horner (2009) comments on the political connotations of the word 'intervention', remarking that intervention indicates the point at which 'powers react to a problem and move to interrupt a set of adverse situations' (p. 246). He also comments that in many social work settings intervention is defined by the employing agency and their procedures, often limiting the range of interventions social workers may actually employ in their practice.

Historical analysis is useful here in terms of recognizing how intervention and assessment are interlinked and shaped by agency procedures. Writers such as Jackson (2000), Ferguson (2004), Payne (2005), Parton (2006 and 2007) and Webb (2007) all provide historical accounts of the development of social work in England and, in doing so, link the development of practice to socio-political pressures and demands through time. Victorian philanthropists intervened by giving time and money to charitable organizations in order to bring about changes to society. The development of child protection practice, for example, took place amid scrutiny into the private lives of families with awareness of how children were being treated, provoking moves toward charity and state intervention to protect children (Ferguson, 2004; Webb, 2007). In America, 'The New York Society for the Prevention of Cruelty to Children' (NYSPCC) was founded in 1875, following the work of social reformists who brought to court the case of a young girl abused by her parents. At the time neither England nor America had laws to protect children, and so animal cruelty laws were used and the reformists, eventually, succeeded in removing the girl from her family. Based on the NYSPCC, the National Society for the Prevention of Cruelty to Children (NSPCC) was founded in England in 1884 and became the principal agency for child protection policy and procedure; it remains very active in bringing about changes and reforms which impact on child protection practice (Ferguson, 2004; Parton, 2007).

In Victorian times emphasis was on intervening to protect children and, as noted in chapter 4, emphasis was not placed on assessment until the middle of the twentieth century. However, implicit within intervention is assessment; in the late 1800s those working for the NSPCC had some notion of childhood, as well as socially constructed ideas of how children 'should' be cared for, and applied these ideas as a measure against which they judged (assessed) those children and circumstances which required intervention. As child protection social work has evolved so, too, have social norms about what is and what is not acceptable care for children. This evolution has led, in the United Kingdom, to a division growing up between the responsibilities of statutory child protection services and those agencies which have developed to fulfil other roles, such as providing parenting support, early intervention or counselling (to name but a few). This division is not necessarily a negative aspect of service provision as it reflects issues of funding, resource allocation and professional expertise. However, what it does highlight is the way in which agency remit has a direct impact on the employing agencies' range of interventions. Therefore, social workers employed in a statutory child protection settings and those in support settings would be expected to have the same core skills, ethical approaches and professional values but would, undoubtedly have access to differing agency resources to support their professional intervention. Child protection has been used here as illustration of how notions of intervention might develop over time, and every agency which employs social workers will have its own history. It is important to consider the wide number of factors which shape employing agencies and how this, in turn, can impact on the 'political' connotations of intervention. For example, agencies focused on more therapeutic interventions will have a different philosophy and approach to intervention than an agency more focused on statutory intervention.

The case study can be used to reflect on how intervention with families can be shaped, and possibly even curtailed, by agency guidance and remit. For example, when assessing and intervening with Maria and Dot, Steve would need to draw on his communications skills (see Chapter 3) to talk about complex issues, particularly in relation to their life and how they wanted to live it given their health needs. To do this, Steve would have needed to quickly develop a trusting relationship which would allow both Maria and Dot, possibly two quite different individuals with different emotional outlooks on life, to feel able to talk about intimate issues. Using Horner's notion that intervention is linked to powers reacting to a problem, the 'problem' can be defined in two ways. Firstly, it might be defined as the agency's problem of managing hospital resources efficiently to ensure people do not remain in hospital beyond the point at which they are medically fit to be discharged. Alternatively, it might be defined as the service user's problem in terms of how they access appropriate services or make changes to their own life and circumstances in order to achieve the outcomes they want. Steve's responsibility is to intervene on behalf of his agency remit as well as on behalf of Maria and Dot.

Identifying the beginning and end of intervention: the influence of hard and soft features

Understanding when intervention is required, or should begin, is important in ensuring service users receive the support they need when they need it. Likewise, recognizing when intervention should end ensures resources are used appropriately and people do not receive services which intrude into their lives unnecessarily. For example, a child experiencing physical abuse should not wait until an assessment is completed before intervention to reduce the risks they face occurs. Also, a parent who has improved their parenting skills sufficiently should not be subject to on-going and intrusive social work intervention. However, identifying beginning and end points is not always a simple issue and may be influenced by many things, including 'hard' factors such as agency policy and procedure or less tangible issues such as workload management or agency thresholds. Similarly, 'soft' features such as emotional engagement may affect the length of time that individual social workers hold a case, workers often inclining towards working with people who are easy to engage with and away from those who are challenging or aggressive. Reflective practice is important when considering the beginning and end of interventions because it enables social workers to understand how their knowledge of the 'hard' and 'soft' features of social work may influence what they are doing and why.

Rather like assessment, social work intervention is shaped by the legislative, policy and procedural frameworks that apply to the practice area. So for example, a social worker practising in a drug rehabilitation service would need awareness of criminal law and the potential legal sanctions used against those accessing the service as well as law, policy and procedures linked to treatment and rehabilitation. In addition, a good working knowledge of legislation and policy relevant to housing, homelessness, financial benefits, access to medical treatment is necessary in order to intervene to ensure appropriate access to resources. In Chapter 1, the authors identified the legal, policy and procedural framework as the 'hard' features of practice, and, certainly, knowledge of these 'hard' features is important in order to frame intervention and to help in the recognition of where social work responsibility begins and ends. However, the 'hard' features are only part of the equation: "soft' features linked to emotions and values are also of significance, not least because feelings towards individuals will influence willingness to offer support and intervention.

Identifying the beginning and end of intervention is a constant issue in social work because there is always a need to control the expenditure of finite and often scarce resources. In *Ethics and values in social work* (2012), Banks considers the bureaucratic environment of social work and questions the inherent tensions such an environment creates in relation to resource allocation. He suggests that being a reflective and reflexive social worker is vital in order to question and challenge bureaucratic systems and rules which, if followed without question, may lead to practitioners acting as technical followers rather than critical thinkers. For example, *Reshaping Care for Older People* (Scottish Government, 2012) clearly identifies the tensions inherent within service provision for vulnerable people between the importance of providing high-quality care that meets individuals' needs and the available services and limited social care budget. *Reshaping Care for Older People* also provides a platform to support thinking about some of the complexities of deciding which service is the most appropriate to offer support, where resources should be allocated and how services should (or could) work together. Social workers are not the only resource available; they usually work with, and in many cases co-ordinate, multi-agency support packages. It is, therefore, important to understand the 'hard' features of social work as a basis for determining which service has a responsibility or obligation to provide resources. However, although the 'hard' features may direct funding resources and shape statutory obligations, the human aspect of working with vulnerable people is far more complex. Identifying when interventions should start and

Reflective Activity 5.2

In a practice setting consider the language used by other professionals in relation to a service user.

1. Does the language used convey positive feelings of warmth, kindness or affection for the service user (e.g. she/he is 'nice' 'friendly' 'chatty' 'sweet' etc.), or feelings of anxiety, anger or dislike (e.g. she/he is aggressive, annoys me, frightens me)?
2. Do the professionals' feelings shape interventions either with regard to access to resources, physical access to buildings, attendance at meetings and so on? What might the consequences of professionals' feelings toward them be for the service user?

end also requires social workers to understand how their own feelings and emotions may be impacting on interventions and resource allocation as well as how the feelings of others, including other professionals, may have an impact on individuals and situations.

Parker and Bradley (2010) consider social work theory, models methods, and how they can inform and shape intervention. In doing so, they demonstrate that intervention is not something that sits alone from the theoretical underpinning of practice. Likewise, Wilson et al. (2011) argue that in order to intervene effectively, social workers must have a solid grasp of theoretical concepts. Using theory to understand intervention approaches is very useful, particularly when trying to establish appropriate end points for intervention. For example, in the case study, Tracy may take a systems approach (see Payne, 2005) to Dot and her daughters and in so doing would consider the impact of social structures and the kind of help available. This may then lead to Tracy updating Steve's assessment of the home care package identified by Steve and so commission additional services into the home. This might reduce the fears of Dot's daughters and so support Dot in her wish to remain at home. Such an approach would open the door to longer-term intervention as there is no identified end because Dot's daughters' fears have not been reduced but responded to. Alternatively, Tracy may take a Task Centred approach (See Dole and Marsh, 1992), identifying goals set by Dot and working with her to set out the steps needed to achieve them. Task-centred practice is useful for resolving areas of concern by working in partnership with people to achieve the desired goal. In Dot's case this may involve working with her to help her daughters understand and accept the risks she wishes to take.

The use of reflective tools and models identified in Chapters 1 and 2 can facilitate this process by promoting methods of thinking and questioning one's own practice. For example, questions such as those in Box 2.4 should also be asked in relation to interventions. This should facilitate questioning the underlying assumptions of why an intervention is necessary, how and why individuals are responding in a certain way to an intervention, as well as questioning the impact of wider influencing factors such as agency policy and procedure. In turn, this should lead to more reflexive approaches to interventions, incorporating Fook and Gardner's (2007) idea that reflexivity requires being able to see what we might not normally see.

Reflective practice enables social workers to identify their preferred method of intervention and the ways that this may impact on how a situation is assessed and responded to. Taylor and White (2006) indicate that in some situations the 'right' answer is clear but for the majority of social work practice the 'right' answer could be one of many plausible options. Therefore, in order to become effective, flexible and creative practitioners, social workers need to employ reflective and reflexive thinking to avoid arriving at definite and prescribed 'right' answers without due consideration of the uncertainties that surround individuals' lives and circumstances (Taylor and White, 2006).

Supervision is an invaluable support when it comes to identifying when, how or if interventions should end because, as Ingram (2012a) suggests, there is a direct link between emotions and decision-making which can be explored in supervision. By using the reflective elements of supervision, analysis of the 'hard' and 'soft' features of a case can take place. In the case studies used in this and the previous chapter, supervision may be used in different ways by Steve and Tracy. For Steve, his intervention has a distinct ending, defined by the remit of the agency, and so for him supervision may need to be focused on how *his* emotional responses to Maria and Dot's situations may result in him over- or under-emphasizing the need for provision of services. Featherstone (2010) considers the ethics of care and points out that caring requires more than good intentions. He argues that caring and helping people is complex: an emotional experience which has received all too little ethical and moral consideration in the social work literature. Reflection on the thoughts, feelings, emotions and values for Steve may, therefore, prompt consideration of how his desire to help Maria and Dot is constrained by the bureaucratic systems surrounding his intervention and how this may, in turn, impact on his assessment of what interventions are required post-discharge. Such tension can in turn lead to ethical stress and, as highlighted by Fenton (2013), professional disjuncture. Tracy's supervision may need to focus much more on how Dot and her daughters make Tracy feel and how that might influence what Tracy regards as an appropriate approach. Supervision is, therefore, a valuable space for reflecting on what exactly is shaping the types of interventions provided, the impact of interventions on the service user their family and even on the social worker.

Intervention and anti-oppressive practice

Beckett (2010) draws a distinction between interventions which require the social worker to get involved at the request of service users, and interventions which are not necessarily wanted by the family; child and adult protection being the most obvious examples. In child or adult protection work the point at which a protective intervention begins is often prompted by an incident or series of incidents which leave an individual at risk of harm and may end when the risk is prevented or mitigated. In such situations, as highlighted by Mattison (2000), procedurally driven practice can often seem attractive to practitioners, particularly if they feel under pressure to act correctly. Procedures provide a framework and may even carry statutory powers to enable intervention. For student social workers and newly qualified social workers, this may seem attractive as it minimizes the need for deep understanding of the situation. However, Hodson (2011), writing about pre-birth assessment, highlighted that the application of child protection legislation and procedure is not possible pre-birth because the foetus does not have the status of personhood. Building on this Hodson and Deery (2014) consider inter-professional ethics in relation to pre-birth assessment and argue that professionals work within extremely complex legal and procedural constructs which they must understand if interventions are to be ethical and effective. Therefore, whilst it is very important to build knowledge around the procedures in order to ensure people are protected, the way in which the procedures are used with individuals has a direct impact on the effectiveness of interventions. Reflection on emotional aspects of practice is of paramount importance in order to understand how someone might be feeling and how they might respond. Emotional intelligence is supremely important to ensure professional responses to vulnerable and sometimes angry people who find themselves at a point of crisis, identify appropriate levels of intervention, and to be able to identify when and how to end intervention appropriately and safely.

To act effectively and anti-oppressively in social work it is essential to reflect on the complexities of what constitutes professional intervention (Ferguson, 2005; Horwath, 2011). In the case study, for example, Steve had clearly spent time listening to Dot's wishes and fears as part of his assessment and so supported her making her own decisions about where she wanted to live; in addition, he intervened to establish an appropriate support package. Tracy then needed to intervene by implementing the supports called for in Steve's assessment and then re-evaluating the situation in line with Dot's daughters' views about their mother being safer in residential care. Once again this shows that assessment and intervention are cyclical in nature.

Ferguson (2005) is clear that working with aggressive or confrontational people may impact on social workers' responses to situations, and although Dot's daughters' approaches may not be physically threatening towards Tracy, it is still important to recognize that they may be aggressive in the sense of being forceful and dogmatic in their views on what outcomes they want for Dot. In turn this may result in Tracy feeling that persuading Dot to accept the views of her daughters may be the 'easier' and 'safer' option in terms of case management and the time needed to be spent with the family. Clearly such an approach is not consistent with anti-oppressive practice, which would place Dot's wishes and feelings at the centre of any intervention. Similarly, Tracy's personal life may also impact on what she defines as appropriate intervention, for example she may also be a carer for her mother and so may identify more with the daughters' perspectives rather than Dot's.

Intervening with families requires social workers to recognize how to manage or control a particular situation or set of circumstances in order to ensure the wellbeing and safety of service users. It is, therefore, important to understand the softer aspects of practice in order to reflect on how they shape and direct social work interventions. In the case study for example, Tracy may totally agree with Dot's daughters and be quite fearful for Dot's wellbeing, and so her interpretation of intervention which improves the situation may be to 'persuade' Dot to move into residential care. However, as the International Federation of Social Workers (IFSW, 2013) statement of ethical principles asserts, issues of dignity, social justice and professional integrity are central to practice. Social workers are required to act compassionately toward those they work with, and act ethically in relation to decision making and actions. This requires an ability to reflect on the complexity of practice, recognition that personal values may shape intervention, and an understanding of the emotional impact of interventions on individuals, families, other professionals and, of course on themselves.

Reflective Activity 5.3

Identify and list the range of interventions you are involved with in one week. These may be interventions which require you to directly provide a service, or indirect interventions (such as managing a care package or attending meetings). Once you have devised your list look at each intervention individually and identify the 'hard' features relevant to law, policy and procedure which shape your interventions. Then identify the 'soft' features you drew upon on, in order to ensure your intervention was effective. Now consider how you felt in relation to each intervention. This will require you to think about feelings perhaps linked to your fear or discomfort with certain people or in certain situations as well as feelings linked to liking or feeling comfortable with someone or something. Finally consider how the 'hard' and 'soft' features shaped and informed your intervention.

Applying the reflective practitioner models to intervention

Caring for our Future: Reforming Care and Support (Department of Health, 2012) focuses on the importance of professionals who are able to develop trusting relationships with people (regardless of their circumstances). As Parker and Bradley (2010) identified, there are many models of intervention available to social workers to help them understand the theory behind what they do and why.

Argyris and Schön's (1974) proposed models of learning introduced in Chapter 2 can be used to identify intervention which is located in the sphere of rational-technical approach (single loop) and that which is based on ongoing re-assessment of experience and developing an understanding of what happened from the perspective of others (double loop). Developing double-loop thinking skills requires practice but, as Heron (2005) suggests, being able to critically reflect is essential to challenging power dynamics and creating anti-oppressive practice.

Considering the case study above, the law governs and provides the framework for the provision of care services in Dot's own home. This will include legislation designed to protect Dot, legislation which directs agencies to provide services, legislation which covers the health and safety of carers working in Dot's home as well as legislation to support Dot's daughters as carers. Dot sits in the middle of this framework and it is Tracy's professional responsibility to communicate with Dot and intervene appropriately. Employing a single-loop approach to reflection might result in Tracy ignoring Dot's daughters' views and sticking rigidly to the plan identified in the assessment, rationalizing this by arguing the assessment has only recently been completed and therefore 'must' be correct. Alternatively Tracy could ignore Dot's perspective in favour of her daughters, seeing the situation to be one of high physical risk and therefore use legal guidance to 'overrule' Dot's wishes. In either of these two scenarios single-loop reflection would result in Tracy rationalizing her actions as in Dot's best interest without actually giving due consideration to Dot, her daughters or how Tracy was responding to them and the situation.

It is not unusual for there to be competing forces when it comes to intervention. Beckett (2006) points out that social work is not an exact science and it is impossible to intervene appropriately by mechanically applying rules. In the case study, the competing forces are Dot's feelings about remaining at home, and her three daughters who fear for their mother's safety and would like to protect her by having her move to residential care, where they perceive her to be safer. Whilst the authors have chosen an example of intervention linked to an older person, any social work intervention is likely to be undertaken in the context of a wide range of competing factors. For example, pre-birth intervention may require social work skills to help a pregnant woman free herself from a violent relationship, requiring consideration of the positive emotional, financial and physical aspects the relationship provides as well as the risk factors for her and her child associated with domestic violence.

It may well be that differing forces are motivated by valid reasons; in the case study Dot's daughters love their mother and want her to be safe, Dot wants to continue her life independently. In cases of domestic violence, it may be that the violent person is a loving partner when not under the influence of drugs or alcohol. The important point is that the social worker needs to understand and question the different forces, and the values and emotions they prompt in all concerned, including the social worker themselves. Without reflection and insight it is impossible to intervene appropriately, as it is impossible to understand what is prompting the intervention. Double-loop thinking requires the social worker to be cognitively flexible and so think about other's perspectives. This requires active listening to people's views, looking beyond the words they say and considering their rationale, motivation, history and rights. Therefore, when working with someone who holds quite different views or opinions, or when working with someone intimidating or who provokes feelings of dislike, double-loop thinking facilitates recognition of these feelings. In turn, this helps ensure the feelings alone are not what shapes the intervention or that 'hard' features of social work are not used in isolation as the rationale for intervention, but that intervention is considered within a wide context.

Competing pressures may also occur as a consequence of structural requirements, not least of which will be case-load management demands and the scarce resource of social work time. As identified earlier in this chapter, intervention is about the 'doing' of social work, but this entails far more than the direct involvement with service users. As can be seen in other chapters in this book, social workers must undertake a wide range of tasks and be able to engage in reflective practice accordingly. In this sense, reflection on intervention is not something totally distinct and certainly overlaps with, for example, reflecting on writing a report which will have a direct impact on subsequent intervention, or reflecting on risk and individuals' rights to take appropriate risks (see Chapters 6 and 8). However, where reflection on intervention is perhaps most distinct is in relation to the level, intensity or duration of intervention.

It is not unusual for social workers to relate to some individual service users more readily than to others. This is not necessarily a problem as relationships are core to social work and each relationship will be different. However, it is essential to reflect upon the factors at play, both to militate against favouring one service user over another in the allocation of resources, and also to ensure critical analysis of service users' situations. In some circumstances it may even be that the service user is more easy to engage with not because of compatible personality traits but because they are attempting to deceive or hide information from the social worker. Thinking about one's own value base and emotional responses is therefore essential to understanding why one person might seem easier to work with than another.

Conclusion

As has been remarked above, knowledge of the legal policy and procedural framework is important in order in understanding the remit of social work intervention; however the 'softer' features of social work are of paramount importance when considering intervention. The process of 'helping' is complex and in social work requires an understanding of the boundary between care and control, as well as empowerment and disempowerment. Social workers are required to understand when statutory responsibility must be fulfilled even if service users perceive the intervention to be unwelcome. Likewise, social workers need to be able to understand individual needs and circumstances in order to identify when to step in and intervene, and when to step back and allow service users to take control of their own situation. Social workers must, therefore, be able to do much more than merely follow rules and guidance. They must be able to understand the legal, policy and procedural frameworks, but recognize them as the scaffolding within which social work skills exist.

This chapter has shown that intervention relates to all actions which impact on service users' lives and as such covers a wide range of day-to-day activities social workers may be involved with. As a consequence, separating out where intervention starts, and other social work tasks such as assessment ends, is not always a simple matter. Reflective practice and the use of supervision to support reflection are of paramount importance when considering intervention. They are a means of assisting social workers to understand the complexity and effectiveness of what is involved in the important task of social work.

Further resources

Beckett, C. (2010) *Assessment and Intervention in Social Work: Preparing for Practice.*
Demonstrates the inter-connectedness of assessment and intervention and shows why distinction between the two areas is important.

Parker, J. and Bradley, G. (2010) *Social Work Practice: Assessment, Planning, Intervention and Review*, 3rd Edition.
Provides a good understanding of the cyclical process of assessment, planning, intervention and reviewing the intervention.

CHAPTER 6

Making significant risk decisions

This chapter will explore the role critical reflection plays in making risk decisions. With a view to counterbalancing the well documented tendency in social work for risk-averse, rational-technical risk practices (Fenton, 2013), the following points will be examined:

- Defensible risk decisions
- Engaging with risk *and* need
- Critical reflection
- Risks and Rights
- Subjective factors affecting risk assessment.

Erika's Diary (Criminal Justice Worker)

Monday
10.00 *Support and supervision – managers office*
(*note* discuss difficulties with Frank Bell*)
12.30 *Lunch with team*
2.00 *Visit John Grey*
4.00 *Report for Frank Bell for case conference*

Tuesday
9.30 *Reflections on work with John*
10.00 *Write report for MAPPA meeting*
1.30 *Multi Agency Public Protection Arrangements meeting re: John Grey. Police Station. Confirm schedule of visits for when John is released*
4.00 *write up meeting notes*

Wednesday
9.30 Phone calls:
John's Landlord for update
Think about employment for John?
10.00 On Duty for drop-in session
1.30 Visit to Karen Laing

Thursday
10.00 Case Conference: Sally, County Buildings
12.00 Write up case conference notes
2.00 Visit to Derek Paterson

Friday
10.00 Visit John Grey (begin to discuss employment)
2.30 Team meeting (x 5 cases)

Saturday

Sunday

Case Study 6.1

Erika is the social worker for John Grey, a service user in a Criminal Justice Social Work (CJSW) team in an urban area of Scotland. CJSW in Scotland is part of the wider social work department, which is in contrast to the rest of the UK where the probation service undertakes work with offenders. Social workers in the rest of the UK, however, do work in youth justice, and the issues pertaining to risk are transferrable and, in fact, generalizable to all areas of social work where risk is a feature.

John has just been released on parole after serving 6 years for the serious and on-going abuse of a 14 year girl with learning disabilities. He made a connection with the victim through his local church (where he volunteered with the Sunday School). John is 50, unemployed and extremely isolated. He has just secured a tenancy on his own small flat in the city.

As John's liberation date drew nearer, Erika had more contact with him and was instrumental in finding him a short-term place in a hostel, and ultimately his own flat. Erika has always, in her heart of hearts, felt sorry for John. She abhors what he did to his victim, but also finds him to be a very sad and lonely character. She knows he comes from an abusive home and, as a child, spent time in a variety of foster homes and eventually a residential establishment for adolescents. He has never had a relationship with another adult, nor does he have any friends, but has expressed a real desire to join a church again.

Later in the week, Erika has to attend a case conference for Sally, aged 8, who was sexually abused by Frank Bell when he lived next door to her. Frank is now on a probation order, and Erika is struggling to work with him. Although he admits to the offence, he denies he caused any harm and blames Sally for being 'provocative.' Erika finds him arrogant and superior, and is struggling to engage with him. It is difficult for her to 'respect … (his) … values and life choices' (British Association of Social Work: BASW, 2012, p. 8) when his values are at odds with her own to such a degree.

The activities listed in Reflective Activities 6.1 will help the reader reflect on Erika's actions and emotions.

Reflective Activity 6.1

1. What are Erika's duties and priorities in relation to John and Frank? What would you do in a similar situation? Why?
2. What influence might her feelings about John and Frank have on her practice? Why might she be feeling this way?
3. What are her duties in relation to Sally?
4. What might the challenges be in expressing her thoughts within a 'multi agency public protection arrangements' (MAPPA) meeting, case conference or to colleagues in the office, especially in the context of John joining a church?
5. As you read the chapter, reflect on what best practice would look like in these cases.

Defensible risk decisions

The principle of making decisions about risk has, for a significant length of time, centred around the concept of the 'defensible decision' (Kemshall, 2002). A defensible decision is one which a body of co-professionals would have also made in the same circumstances (Carson, 1996) and where a worker can demonstrate that all reasonable steps have been taken in making the decision. Munro (2011) identifies one of the main principles of good risk practice:

> The standard expected and required of those working in child protection is that their risk decisions should be consistent with those that would have been made in the same circumstances by professionals of similar specialism or experience (p. 44).

In order to demonstrate this, workers must be able to show that they have gathered information thoroughly, have taken reasonable and logical steps and have thought clearly and comprehensively in coming to their decision (Kemshall, 2002). In theory, this should mean that decisions themselves can stand up to scrutiny in hindsight, even if something has gone wrong with the case, and even if a tragedy has resulted. However, this is a contested principle and one which is fraught with difficulty. For example, when a tragedy results from a case in which social work has been involved, there is often an assumption that poor practice is the reason for the bad outcome. Littlechild (2010) explores this idea, suggesting that there is inordinate faith placed in the tools of risk assessment, to the extent that if something does go wrong, then it *must* be the worker's fault, probably because of not using the tool properly. Littlechild points out that this destructive way of thinking is exacerbated by the '"actuarial fallacy", that is the false assumption that we can accurately predict who will harm their child or re-offend' (Littlechild, 2010, p. 668). Insurance companies increase payments for people in their 'high risk' group (as do social work departments, with increased visits to those children who are subject to child protection plans, for example) in the knowledge that one or more of the group will inevitably have an accident. They do not, however, try to predict which one, as that would be impossible. Littlechild suggests that in social work's 'high risk' group certain parents will inevitably harm their children, certain offenders will reoffend and certain mental health service-users will harm themselves, but it is not always possible to predict which ones. Social work as a profession needs to accept that reality. As Munro (2011,

p. 38) states, 'It is therefore important to convey a more accurate picture of the work and an understanding that the death or serious injury of a child may follow even when the quality of professional practice is high'.

When there is an unfavourable outcome to a situation in which social workers are involved, government often responds with 'managerialism... which consists of a controlling approach to micro-practice' (Littlechild, 2010, p. 665). This results in social work becoming increasingly risk-averse and in the erosion of social workers' autonomy and discretion to respond in the way they feel is right. Philips (2009) suggests that social workers often feel the fear of taking risk decisions, and something going wrong, more strongly than anything else. He suggests that this leads to an over-reliance on defensible decision making, although he admits that even this is not a defence as, with the wisdom of hindsight, any decision can be viewed as indefensible.

Macdonald and Macdonald (2010) point to an important distinction between risk and uncertainty, in which risk is defined as not having certain knowledge that something will happen, but knowing the odds, and uncertainty is defined as 'not even knowing the odds' (p. 1178). Macdonald and Macdonald give the example of child neglect as a situation of uncertainty, where there are 'unknowns' about many factors, not least the outcomes of one course of action as opposed to another. This means that there is often 'an apparent mismatch between informed effort and success' within which the influence on outcomes of 'large random shocks' should not be underestimated (*ibid.*, p. 1179). As they state, this has implications for the way in which practice is evaluated, with decisions themselves meriting evaluation, uncoupled from the outcome (Macdonald, 1990; Macdonald and Macdonald, 2010). This is at odds with an approach based on certainty derived from actuarial 'tools' and standardized procedures that, with correct usage, are assumed to always lead to good outcomes. Munro (2011) reinforces this idea with explicit attention to the idea of 'uncertainty' in child protection work. In particular, Munro suggests that uncertainty occurs at the assessment stage in identify abuse of harm, and in the intervention stage which involves make future predictions of potential abuse or harm: 'such decisions involve making predictions about likely future harm and so are fallible' (Munro, 2011, p. 13). Decisions themselves, therefore, must be explicitly defensible *but* on-going uncertainty must also be acknowledged as a facet of the work.

It is clear from all of the above, then, that this is still a contested area. On one hand, enquiries are preoccupied with stopping social workers from making 'wrong' decisions (Macdonald and Macdonald, 2010), and, on the other hand, there are calls for more understanding of uncertainty and the reality of practice (Munro, 2011). An international literature review conducted by Barry (2007) into effective approaches to risk assessment found social work departments to be risk-averse and defensive in their practices. She also found that the safety of agencies took priority and that workers were ultimately concerned with showing due diligence in their decisions, in case something went wrong resulting in them being blamed. Barry suggests that these attitudes and procedures were often adopted at the expense of genuinely engaging and working in the best interests of service users.

Against this rather depressing backdrop, then, what can actually be done in practice? There are cultural pressures from agencies to conform to their ways of working which might well be 'safety first', and it would be difficult for any one social worker to stand against such a prevailing culture. So, when Erika attends the MAPPA meeting in relation to John Grey, the concepts discussed above contextualize her work. It would be incumbent upon her to reflect on the extent to which her agency is risk-averse and defensive in its decisions. It would also serve her well to consider Banks's (2006) summing up of social work risk decisions. She states that social work decisions are really dilemmas, that is, there are no clearly right or clearly wrong choices to be made; often the social worker simply has to choose the lesser of two evils. Whichever choice is made, therefore, the possibility of 'evil' is a reality and Erika must choose the one she believes (for good, defensible reasons) to have the best chance of success, and, again, live with the consequent uncertainty.

Attending the meeting, having reflected on, and come to an understanding of, the above concepts and how her agency operates in relation to them, will mean that Erika is in a position of understanding why certain decisions are more attractive to the meeting than others. Her opinions may not be 'wrong' but may well be different from other key players in the meeting whose agendas may be about keeping the agency safe from criticism.

The Management of Offenders (Scotland) Act 2005 and the Criminal Justice Act (2003) define those offenders considered to be 'high risk.' Anyone on the Sexual Offenders Register is deemed to be high risk, and both John and Frank are registered sex offenders.

The Acts are operationalized by MAPPA which is a system of multi-agency case conferences designed to assess risk and manage high-risk offenders. The police and CJSW or the Probation Service attend MAPPA meetings, along with representatives from the Housing Department and other interested parties (Scottish Government, 2007; Ministry of Justice, 2012). Social workers taking part in MAPPA meetings, often chaired by a management member of the police, or by a manager from the Probation Service or criminal justice social work, may possibly feel quite intimidated by their formal nature and the perceived status of others taking part (see Chapter 6). Halliday and co-workers, in a study of report writing by criminal justice social workers in Scotland, found that workers worried that 'their professional discourse of welfare and care would be undervalued as "namby-pambiness"' (Halliday et al., 2009, p. 422). This role ambiguity may also play out in contexts where welfare and care appear to have even less of a place, for example when discussions are concerned with 'dangerous' offenders and 'high-risk' people. In relation to the case study, there is a strong possibility that Erika will find articulating anything concerned with John's *needs* as opposed to *risks,* very difficult within the context of the MAPPA meeting. However, her values may lead her to feel that although it is important to assess and manage his risk properly, a focus on this should not entirely eclipse the social work concern with his needs. Nonetheless, she may find it difficult to imagine how such a subject could be raised in a meeting so fundamentally concerned with the management of a 'risky' person.

In relation to the case conference for Sally, Erika may find that similar issues prevail. The childcare social worker working with Sally may want Frank to be given very restrictive instructions, curtailing his movements around the city, for example. Erika might think this is overly punitive and may feel that lesser restrictions are sufficient. Again, however, the difficulty for any social worker arguing *for* an offender in such an emotionally charged situation is undeniable (see also Chapter 7 for an exploration of some of the

Reflective Activity 6.2

1. Why might Erika find 'reflecting-for-action' easier in terms of John than Frank?
2. Analyse why Erika might feel so differently towards each service user.

dynamics at play within meetings). Also, it is worth considering whether Erika's emotional reaction to Frank may actually incline her to support Frank's wishes to a lesser degree than John's.

Engaging with risk and need

The MAPPA meeting in relation to the case study is likely to review John's standardized risk assessment for sex offenders, RM2000 or other accredited risk assessment tool, which indicates, in actuarial terms, what level of risk an offender poses (Thornton, 2007). The police and Erika would probably set a schedule of visits to monitor John, including unannounced and joint home visits, and review dates would also be set. Clearly, the tasks so far are all concerned with managing the risk.

Erika is likely, at some point, to be asked by the chair to give an account of the work being done and planned with John. At this point, a social worker in a situation like this may employ a 'reflection-in-action' technique (Schon, 1983) and be able to use, for example, emotional intelligence to understand what the priorities of the meeting are (Ingram, 2013). A social worker may also be able to reflect on academic knowledge, social work values (showing respect for John by promoting his interests) and legal and policy directives to arrive at a plan for presenting their thoughts about the case. Erika, therefore, might begin by outlining the risk-management procedures she has in place in her practice with John, in recognition of the risk priorities of the meeting. She may then move onto discussing John's isolation and making clear links to the 'promotion of welfare' imperative in the Social Work (Scotland) Act 1968, and to social work values, for example the BASW principle 'treating each person as a whole' (BASW, 2012, p. 8). As Stanford (2010) points out, risk *and* need are normally present in any one service user, and, reflecting the reality of life, a decision is usually made about which dimension takes priority. Understanding this might help Erika realize that it is, in fact, legitimate to talk about John's needs as well as his risks. She then should be able to discuss John's isolation and the fact that he wants to join a church and thus take steps to be reintegrated into the community.

Erika's point can also be re-framed in terms of risk, by utilizing the knowledge that helping John reintegrate will probably reduce his risk of re-offending. According to the body of research concerned with 'desistance' (that is, a person's own journey out of crime, McCulloch and McNeill, 2008), subjective changes in a person's life which that person values should be supported by services trying to help them refrain from offending. This means that the desistance literature would give an evidence base to a decision to help John join a church. The meeting may well be persuaded that John joining a church is a good decision, and would then begin to look at how to minimize the risk that supporting John to do this would inevitably create. However, the discussion would be about risk *management* as opposed to risk *aversion* or *control*, which attempts to vacuum out all risk (by, usually, denying desired freedoms, Hudson, 2001) and therefore should feel positive to Erika. The meeting might agree, for example, that John would be asked permission for 'disclosure' to the minister, that he will not be permitted to join in any activities involving Sunday School, and that Erika and the minister will remain in contact.

The decision now looks like a defensible one. All reasonable steps have been taken to analyse the index offence, to minimize (but not eradicate) all of the risk factors and to draw up a management plan which is on-going and can be redrawn at any time. John joining the church is, in itself, a risk-minimizing part of the plan, especially given the weight of evidence brought to bear by the desistance literature.

Critical reflection

The above account of a MAPPA, or other interdisciplinary, meeting may well feel familiar to social workers in any setting. In the case study, Erika was able to reflect-in-action successfully. However, for less experienced, or less confident, workers, this may well pose more of a challenge. Thompson and Thompson (2008) discuss 'reflection-for-action' (p. 16) which is the planning or thinking ahead about what may be about to happen. A worker might usefully reflect on the ideas about risk held by their agency, and might be able to successfully plan what they are going to say in the light of this. This would also allow them space and time to work out why what they had to say was important, and why caring about John's needs should not be construed as 'namby-pambiness'. Erika might have, for example, done some reading about need being as important as risk, reflected upon the place of social work values in her work with John, and made links between the desistance literature and what she wanted to do. Her reflection-for-action might have led her to the realization that one of the driving forces in her practice with John is the relationship she has with him. She may well believe that this is the starting point for social work generally, no matter what service-user group is being worked with. As Gregory (2010) states, the experienced probation officers in her study were very clear that building a relationship with the offenders they worked with was absolutely central to their work. Hennessey (2011) also states that building relationships with service users is at the very core of all areas of social work. Erika may feel this instinctively, but knowing the literature and writers around whose views are similar to hers would have given her confidence in this aspect of her own practice.

She may also have investigated the desistance literature more comprehensively and have read Farrall's (2002) integrated theory which states that changes in an offender's life which that person values should be the target for support work, regardless of whether the issues are directly related to the offence or not. Therefore, family relationship work, housing, employment or anything else highlighted by the offender is a legitimate area of work. This might help validate Erika's endeavour to build a relationship with John and to address whatever needs he identifies as important. Even if it remains difficult to articulate this in a MAPPA meeting, Erika would have her evidence-based argument prepared, and would be able to express why she wanted to do the work with John which she did.

Risks and rights

In relation to the case conference concerned with Sally, it is possible that Erika's learning from the MAPPA meeting and reflection on how things went would encourage her to reflect-for-action in preparation for the conference. She may have been reflecting-on-action and crystallizing in her own mind the view that there seems to be an enduring tension between encouraging the rehabilitation of offenders by helping service users with that endeavour and helping with their lives more generally, and social work's preoccupation with risk. She may begin to realize that with decisions to support desistance or to help offenders with welfare comes anxiety, and this seems to be where one of the difficulties lie. In order that no anxiety is produced, social workers would have to practise extremely risk-aversely, allow service users to take no risks, to try nothing in terms of rehabilitation and, in fact, simply say 'no' all of the time. In terms of values, including the belief that people can change and that we should respect people and promote their rights, this would probably cause Erika significant discomfort.

Taylor (2007) describes the anxiety experienced by social workers who try to do the 'right' thing as opposed to the 'safe' thing by practising in a narrow, procedural or managerial way, as 'ontological anxiety,' and states that it should be considered as a natural and healthy consequence of good, responsive social work practice. (Taylor, 2007, p. 94). As explored earlier, Barry (2007) found that agencies were indeed practising in a 'safe' managerialist manner, which might reduce resultant ontological anxiety, but does not provide the context for responsive, relationship-based practice. Sawyer (2009) in a study of mental health workers, interviewed a social worker who consistently ignored a policy which stated workers should not intervene with service users who were under the influence of substances. The worker felt the policy overlooked individual circumstances, the relationship with the service user and the service user's vulnerability. The worker created ontological anxiety for himself (which Taylor would state was proper and healthy) by intervening in the way he felt was 'right' but, by doing so, shouldered the entire risk of something going wrong. The agency would be able to honestly state that he had not followed procedure. This is a good example of the anxiety created by 'risk-accepting' practice, which, although healthy according to Taylor, might be anathema to any worker who worries about risk decisions and things going wrong (Philips, 2009). It also exemplifies, however, how far some workers will go to avoid the feelings of disjuncture which, in this case, would be created by the worker not involving himself with a vulnerable service user who needed his help. The worker in this case, however, had to make that decision and work alone, without agency support. A policy like this, then, which controls workers in such a risk-averse and managerial way, may well put workers in the most difficult of positions, and this worker chose active resistance at his own expense.

What, then, might counterbalance the social work tendency for anxiety-reducing, risk-averse practice? As already discussed, the desistance literature, social work values and legal duties to promote welfare can all go some way to resisting it, and, in addition, further reflection might pave the way for consideration of human rights. Hudson (2001) discusses the importance of social work embracing a 'positive human rights agenda' (Hudson, 2001, p. 110) which promotes the minimum intervention commensurate with public security, and the maximum protection of the offender's human rights. This, therefore, means that anything which can be done to promote inclusion and reintegration should be an explicit part of the discussion and work done (Fenton, 2013). Again this may not be easy in the context of a MAPPA meeting, in a criminal justice agency more broadly or in any context where risk decisions are being made, but understanding the thinking should give a social worker increased confidence.

So, in relation to the case study, Erika may feel more confident about protecting the maximum amount of Frank's rights congruent with the minimum restriction required to protect Sally and other victims from risk. It is important for any social worker to introduce the discussion about what the maximum amount of rights would actually look like in practice. For John it might mean attending a church as well as other social activities; for Frank it might mean freedom to travel wherever he wishes to. It may be that those freedoms are ultimately curtailed after discussion because they fail to meet the minimum requirement for the protection of other people, but the social worker will have demonstrated best practice by raising the issues as important discussion points. If Erika, because of fears that her discussion of John's interests would be viewed as 'namby-pambiness', or because she wanted to please her service manager by being seen as a 'strong' social worker only concerned with risk, had decided not to discuss John's desire to join a church, or had acquiesced to the childcare social worker's restrictive instructions even whilst disagreeing that Frank required them, she may well have suffered feelings of 'disjuncture'. The experience of disjuncture is one that many, if not all, social workers have experienced at some time. Using the strength of that feeling to reflect honestly on one's values/action incongruence can lead to productive redress of the issues causing the 'disjuncture.' In effect, the conscious recognition of the feeling of 'disjuncture' can be used as a guide for value-based practice.

Munro (2011) contextualizes all of the above in the ten principles of 'risk-sensible' practice (p. 60). The principles include taking decisions in uncertain conditions, balancing harms and benefits, judging risk decisions by the decisions themselves rather than by the outcomes, creating a culture of learning from both successes and failures and sharing information. And, of course, achieving the safety of people is a priority consideration. We can see those principles play out in Erika's practice with both service users, and can

Reflective Activity 6.3

1. Reflect on a significant risk decision you have been part of. Was a 'positive human rights' framework adopted? If not, how *would* it have changed the discussion?
2. In terms of decisions about risk, are there other issues which are ignored due to fear of being perceived as 'namby-pamby' or due to the fear of anxiety?

also see how important it is that she uncover the internal processes underlying and influencing that practice.

Subjective factors affecting risk assessment

The relationship with the service user is central to any social work interaction. In the case of social work decisions about risk, however, it is something that can sometimes be de-prioritized in the face of requirements for public protection and standardized risk measures. As Gregory (2010) states, in relation to her research with experienced probation officers: 'the kind of practice in which the participants are involved requires them to find connections to others who have sometimes done some terrible things, and they are clear about their responsibility to continue to do this, even if a technical solution could be applied' (p. 2284). Gregory's conclusion is that the processes of critical reflection and reflexivity are the tools required by a worker to resist the extremes of technicist and managerial practices, and to continue to understand the importance of relationship building and meeting the needs of service users.

Furthermore, really knowing the service user well is a prerequisite to undertaking a tailored risk assessment which properly considers the individual person and all their circumstances; in other words, going beyond the standard risk-assessment tools to the consideration of the person and the environment (McNeill et al., 2005). The social worker must build a relationship with the service user in order to be able to ask him or her difficult questions and create a culture where the offender can talk openly. Communication and relationship-building are vital so that assessments are thoroughly individualized and not solely based on commonalities and shared profiles (see also Chapters 3 and 4). Munro (2011) echoes this and states that, in relation to child protection work, social workers must 'create a relationship where the parent is willing to tell you anything… (and know) how to ask challenging questions' (p. 87). By reflecting on all of this, Erika would have been able to discuss her relationships with John and Frank, and the legitimate work involved in getting to know them, with any colleague or manager who feels she is wasting her time and should be involved in technical management only. Erika would need to have a well-thought out and reflective stance on this, knowing that the evidence and current literature about the importance of building relationships gives her argument credence.

The values dimension of the work with John and Frank, and the role values play in risk decisions more broadly, are important areas for critical reflection. Once again, Erika must know the value basis of her reflections, feelings and actions, in order to remain a critically reflective and reflexive practitioner. In her work with both service users, Erika should be able to trace her practice back to the first principles of social work values. In both cases, as already stated, 'treating each person as a whole' (BASW, 2012, p. 8) legitimizes Erika moving the discussion beyond risk factors to a holistic consideration of each service user, including their needs, rights and wants. The BASW principle concerned with risk spells out that social workers must 'recognize that people using social work services have the right to take risks and should enable them to identify and manage potential and actual risk, while seeking to ensure that their behaviour does not harm themselves or other people' (p. 12). Once again, then, working in accordance with the value base of social work means that workers must discuss the difficult balance of rights and risks. Erring on the side of risk control and not discussing rights, freedom and risk-taking leads to poor, oppressive practice, an erosion of human rights and, possibly, 'disjuncture' for the worker.

As already stated, Erika feels quite sorry for John in relation to his early life and his current lonely existence. She also, however, feels very differently towards Frank, and actually may well dislike him. What impact might these factors have on her practice? To practice reflexively, Erika must understand her place in the reflective process and must remain self-aware. Ingram (2013) draws attention to 'impression management' (p. 12), a concept concerned with individual social workers presenting themselves in whichever acceptable way the situation calls for. So, for Erika, who is masking emotions of dislike and aversion towards Frank, reflexive practice would involve an awareness of those feelings, processes and of the impact upon her practice. She would also need a supportive forum for discussion and exploration of those feelings. Supervision would be one such forum, and would rely not only on the worker reflecting upon those feelings and identifying them as important for discussion, but also on supervision allowing space and time for such discussion (see Chapter 9).

Beddoe (2010) explains that the literature surrounding supervision gives a strong message that open debate, trust and supportive discussion which encourages critical reflection on things that have gone wrong and on emotional impact of the work is an optimum for supervision. She further explains, however, that this is difficult if, within a risk-averse climate 'the nagging concerns of risk, fear and accountability crop up in the space between the participants' (Beddoe, 2010, p. 1292). In a supervisory relationship which helps workers contain anxiety and allows for open and honest discussion, the discussion of emotions, both positive and negative, would be encouraged (see Chapter 9 for more on supervision).

A social worker who can identify their emotions as important to the relationship with the service user will be able to make use of the supervisory context to make sense of, and understand, the impact their emotions may be having on the work. Furthermore, as Ingram (2013) states, social workers should be able to 'meaningfully explore, *use* and record [their emotions]' (p. 16, emphasis added). Recognizing, and discussing the social worker's emotions might lead to reflection on the underlying basis for the feelings. For Erika, are there certain aspects of Frank's offence which are deeply troubling? Are there any current behaviours or warning signs from him which Erika is picking up? Is she avoiding building a relationship with Frank because she dislikes him? Why does Erika feel sorry for John? What is it about his life that troubles and saddens her? Can she use this to sharpen the focus on his needs? Exploring these

Reflective Activity 6.4

1. Talk to a colleague about a time when the relationship with a service user was more important to you than usual.
   a. Why was that the case?
   b. Were you more likely to take risks for this person?
2. Ask your colleague to share a similar story. Between you, really try to analyse why you felt the way you did. Pay particular attention to emotions and values.

questions might uncover aspects of both cases which may other-wise have been left undetected and she will be able to work more effectively as a reflexive practitioner.

Conclusion

Legislation, policy and theoretical evidence are 'given' in terms of the model outlined in Chapter 1. The central features of the current chapter relate to the individually tailored aspects of a social work interaction, namely the relationship with the service user and the reflection, values and emotions surrounding both the relationship and social work encounter. When the encounter is centrally concerned with risk, the opportunities for risk-averse, defensive and, ultimately, oppressive practice abound. Therefore, it is crucial that social workers are prepared to engage in critical reflection in terms of risk priorities, rights versus risks, the relationship the worker has with the service user (good or bad), how their practice relates to social work values (congruent or disjunctive?) and what part their emotions are playing in the interaction.

In relation to the case study above, Erika's reflections and dilem-mas are highlighted as common features of any risk decision-making practice which embraces a social work approach beyond the rational-technical application of tools and procedures. The anxiety that such an approach inevitably produces is also high-lighted as a consequence which, although positive, must be contained and worked with. Such is the real nature of working with risk in social work.

Further resources

Barry, M. (2007) *Effective Approaches to Risk Assessment In Social Work: An International Literature Review.*
Provides an overview of risk trends within social work.

Hudson, B. (2001) 'Human rights, public safety and the probation service: defending justice in the risk society', *The Howard Journal*, 40, 103–113.
Read for some thought-provoking ideas about human rights and working with those who might pose a risk.

CHAPTER 7
Meetings

This chapter looks at the reflective process in social work meetings. What are the specific features of a meeting that impact on work practices and why do social workers need a reflexive awareness of them? This chapter will explore:

- the meeting: a particular context
- group dynamics and knowledge
- power dynamics
- strategies in meetings

Susan's Diary (Care Manager)

Monday
9.30 Visit occupational therapy team (remember to ask for lumber roll)
Catch up on minutes of last Friday's meeting
Send agenda out for 21st January meeting
Ask Tim for feedback on home visit

Tuesday
9.00 Team Meeting
1.00 Phone Salim to organize care for Mrs Farmington

Wednesday
Phone calls:
Elsie's son, Kelly family, Harold Sinclair and follow up work
2.30 Meeting with Elsie prior to the discharge meeting (note* remember to talk to the nursing staff while on the ward)
3.30 Write report for Elsie's discharge meeting

Thursday
10.00 Discharge meeting: Elsie Tanworth, Ward 4 meeting room
12.00 Lunch in town
1.30 Meeting with Mary Hendry and family.
3.00 Report writing

Friday
10.00 Supervision session with Harry
3.00 Admin tasks
Make notes for Support and Supervision next week.

Saturday

Sunday

Case Study 7.1

Susan is the care manager for Elsie Tanworth (86). Elsie lives at home, in the house she has lived in for 45 years, but two weeks ago had a fall and broke her hip, which led to her admission to hospital. Elsie suffers from early-stage dementia which manifests itself in problems with her memory. She loses things, forgets to pay bills and sometimes forgets to go shopping or to eat regularly. She has some support from family members, but lost her husband seven years previously, and so is alone for much of the time.

Susan has a good relationship with Elsie and is aware that remaining in her own home is of utmost importance to her. She also knows that the loss of her husband was devastating for Elsie and that she can feel very lonely and depressed. Elsie has refused to attend the local day centre or to accept meals-on-wheels or domestic help, insisting that she is 'managing fine.' Since her fall, her mobility is somewhat compromised, although she can still get around. Going out for shopping or social visits will be more problematic.

The discharge meeting is being held at the hospital, and Susan knows that the medical staff think Elsie needs far more support. They think she should consider residential care as things are only going to get worse. Elsie's son cannot attend the meeting, but Susan knows he would be quite happy for his mother to be well cared for in a residential establishment. He has not been able to voice this to her, however. Susan is aware that the consultant geriatrician, senior nursing staff and the occupational therapist will be at the meeting.

The questions listed in Reflective Activity 7.1 will help the reader reflect on the case study.

Reflective Activity 7.1

1. Susan will want to 'reflect-for-action' prior to the meeting. What might be the subject of her reflections?
2. In anticipation of the meeting, what might be her main worries?
3. What ethical dilemmas might Susan reflect upon?
4. Think about any experience you have of anticipating a meeting where you knew you were expected to contribute. How did you feel? What did you think about?

The meeting: a particular context

Chapter 2 made a clear distinction between reflection and reflexivity by describing reflection as a process and reflexivity as a particular stance in relation to that process. Reflexivity is characterized by the awareness of self in the process of reflection – the unique contribution and impact of one's own presence in the situation. This is, of course, important in any social work interaction, and in the process of reflection upon that particular interaction. The importance of reflexivity in relation to a multi-member meeting is, however, arguably even more important, as the dynamics experienced, caused, reshaped or affected by our *self* may be less obvious and more easily hidden than in a one-to-one interaction. And yet, Doel (2006) states that issues relating to power dynamics may be *more* obvious within a group work setting, such as a meeting. These two points of view can be reconciled by an understanding that issues of power may be exaggerated in a meeting, which may, in turn, cause participants in the meeting to be less likely to contribute critically and more likely to conform. A lack of reflexivity in relation to oneself succumbing to those power issues, may lead to unthinking allegiance with the group and its decisions. As Fook (2012, p. 49) states:

> To take a reflexive stance, you need to be able to appreciate how your own self and *social position* (i.e. your own subjective context) influences your thinking and actions...An ability to identify and analyse the influence of context is therefore intertwined with the ability to reflect and be reflexive. (emphasis added)

Before looking at the reflexivity necessary for good social work practice within a meeting, therefore, an analysis of the context is necessary, because, according to Fook, understanding the context is central to the reflective process. The background to understanding the particular context of a meeting must include an understanding of some of the main features of the organization within which the meeting operates as part of the decision-making function of that organization. As Mullender and Perrott (2002) note, statutory social work often lacks the autonomy available to professionals within other sectors, for example medicine, and is subject to a significant degree of legislative, policy and procedural regulation. This means that meetings often operate as part of the procedural functioning of the organization. It can, therefore, be seen that a technical-rational approach to social work per se, might well impact on the functioning of meetings in that there may be little space for reflection, recognition of emotions and value issues, and a predominance of technical-rational reliance on tools, procedures and accountability measures.

Pagliari and Grimshaw (2002) sum up the key messages from literature on dynamics that affect performance in meetings as follows: the group's performance will be affected by the interaction of its members; group members can be influenced by pressure to conform from the majority of members or influential individuals; the status of any individual affects the influence that person has; and how much verbal input a person has will also depend on their status. Tying both of these elements together, then, it can be seen that Fook's imperative for understanding the context in order to be able to reflect properly during meetings, begins with an understanding of organizational technical-rationality (See Chapter 1) and of interprofessional group dynamics.

Group dynamics and knowledge

One of Susan's reflections, prior to the meeting, might be that she feels nervous and intimidated by the fact that senior medical staff will be present. She might also be aware that they have a different opinion to hers, and that this might make it difficult to speak out. As mentioned above, Pagliari and Grimshaw (2006) found that the status a person is *perceived* to have will, within a meeting, affect how influential they are and how much they contribute. Susan's worries are, therefore, not without basis. She may think that she will probably not contribute much, because, even although she knows Elsie well and understands what Elsie wants, she is aware she lacks the medical and technical knowledge held by the consultant. An inquiry into the death of 11-week-old Caleb Ness, who died due to his father violently shaking him, found a similar dynamic when a nurse who disagreed with the optimistic view of the case conference that Caleb should go home, especially if his father was involved in the care, did not voice her concerns assertively enough. The report states:

> We believe that Nurse 1 may have been too tentative in the way that she phrased her concerns, and she accepted in evidence to us that she did not stick to her guns and insist on further discussion

of her view that Caleb should not be permitted to go home at all. She told us that at the time she was relatively new to Case Conferences, and had received no training about them' (O'Brien, 2003, p. 51).

Fook (2012) points out that modern notions of knowledge have tended to prioritize theoretical knowledge as 'expert' when considered alongside practical knowledge. This has been a mechanism for 'legitimizing professional power' (Fook, 2012, p. 51) and its influence can be discerned in the example above and in the case study. The nurse in the example above felt 'new' and was unable to put her concerns assertively to the case conference, based as they were on practical knowledge and observations. This, perhaps, felt inferior to the theoretical and process knowledge held by the 'experts' in the group. An added difficulty for the nurse might also have been the emergence of 'groupthink,' a drive towards group consensus without proper consideration of alternatives, also known as 'the rule of optimism' (Calder, 2003, p. 40). Gambrill (2012, p. 489) defines groupthink as 'overlooking deficits in a preferred view because of a lack of consideration of disadvantages and well-argued alternatives'. The 'groupthink' in the above example was towards Caleb returning home safely. Negative information which contradicted this optimistic view was either missing or downplayed quite significantly, e.g. the father's head injury, the nurse's concerns, the mother's entrenched drug misuse, and the lack of clarity about who exactly would be caring for Caleb. The case conference reached a conclusion about Caleb going home without any person actually naming that course of action as an agreed decision, such was the assumptive power of the 'groupthink.' This is an example with a tragic outcome, but one which also powerfully illustrates how certain features of a meeting can influence direction and decision making in a dangerous way. Hence the even more pressing need for reflection and reflexivity on the dynamics and processes.

These group dynamics can also be applied to the case study. As stated, Susan might feel that her knowledge of Elsie, gained through their relationship, is somehow less important than the consultant's theoretical knowledge of dementia and risk. There might also be an emerging 'groupthink' about the unquestioned inevitability of Elsie moving to a residential provision. Information in contradiction of this might well be downplayed, especially if voiced tentatively by a social worker who feels intimidated. Devitt, Philip and McLachlan (2010) found that in multi-disciplinary meetings with health professionals to discuss cancer care, allied health professionals felt 'inhibited when offering their contribution' (p. 19). The authors draw on literature which suggests that well known group members, and group members who have information in common with other group members, are often the most influential in a meeting. They use this theory to explain the difficulty experienced by allied health professionals in contributing their, often unique, information. Once again, the majority or 'expert' opinion appears to be considered the most valuable in the decision-making process and often shapes the consequent groupthink. Calder (2003) gives responsibility to the chairperson to challenge groupthink by making sure that questions are asked of everyone, regardless of status, and encouraging and valuing differences of opinion, but this must be supplemented by individual group members feeling able to contribute equally. Fook (2012) considers that a postmodern stance can be helpful in situations such as this, by the denial that one type of knowledge should be privileged over another. She states that postmodernism upsets hierarchical views of knowledge and, thus, values everyone's contribution in recognition of the complexity of the situation and differing perspectives. It might help Susan to be aware of this type of thinking when she reflects-for-action (Thompson and Thompson, 2008) prior to the meeting. Susan would also benefit from understanding the roots of her fears about contributing through an understanding of the status and hierarchical dynamics at play.

Reflective Activity 7.2

1. Susan needs to develop a reflexive understanding of the roots of her ideas and feelings about status. Where might they come from? What messages and assumptions about status might Susan have grown up with?

2. Think about your own beliefs and assumptions about status. What does status mean to you? How might these assumptions influence your behaviour in meetings and in general?

3. Think of a meeting you attended recently. Draw a rough sketch using symbols for the participants. Make a note of which kind of knowledge each member contributed. Did certain knowledge have priority? Why? Did certain people with knowledge *not* speak out? Why might that have been? Analyse your own contribution in terms of knowledge and perceived status.

Given all of the above, then, and taking into account Fook's imperative for understanding the context within which the social worker is operating, how does a worker begin to think reflexively about her or his place and importance in the meeting and decision-making process?

Power dynamics

Power dynamics might be usefully considered in terms of the experience of meetings from service users' point of view. Ghaffar, Manby and Race (2012) undertook a study of parents' experiences inside the child protection system and found that most parents in their study were intimidated and daunted by the experience of attending a child protection case conference. They also found that most parents had real difficulty in contributing to the meeting on an equal basis with the professionals in attendance, whose strength in numbers was an added concern. For example, one parent in the study said that she did not have a chance 'to give my point of view. I did try... but I never talked... there were so many people' (Ghaffar et al., 2012, p. 898). Thinking about this comment in relation to Palgliari and Grimshaw's (2006) finding that influential members with high status, and opinions held by the majority of group members have the most sway within a meeting, it is easy to see that parents, both outnumbered and surrounded by 'professionals' of varying status, might find it very difficult indeed to contribute. In addition, the prioritization of 'expert' knowledge over 'lived' or practical knowledge, as already discussed, also contributes to the 'down-ranking' of the parents. Use of technical or jargonistic phrases and references to theory may well be viewed as 'expert' and valued over what the parent knows and understands about the situation. The location of the meeting, for example in a service user's home as opposed to a more formal setting such as a hospital meeting room, might also affect power dynamics (See also Chapter 3).

The above analysis is ultimately concerned with power dynamics. It is clear that parents do not feel equal in terms of power, and it is also clear that different group members feel different levels of power depending on status, knowledge contribution, congruence of opinions with the majority opinion and the influence of group issues such as groupthink. With an awareness of this particular context, shaped by those features, a social work practitioner might begin to reflect on issues of power. According to Fook and Askeland (2006, p. 44) 'This is one of the functions of critical reflection, to enable awareness of one's own use of power. Another function of critical reflection is to enable changed actions based on these new insights about the operation of power.' In other words, Fook and Askeland urge social workers to deconstruct notions of power, hierarchy and authority *in order* that they be constructed. In any meeting context, it is the job of the social worker to engage in critical reflection of the power dynamics so as to facilitate a reconstruction that allows for more power to be exercised by the service users involved. It is at this juncture that reflexivity is important, in order to understand our own ability to take action or create influence and to be explicitly aware of our reactions to, and effect on, the immediate context. In other words, we need an awareness of the power we hold to be able to empower others.

Fook (2012) discusses findings of a study she undertook where workers defined themselves as powerless, subject to the power of managers, supervisors, procedures, bureaucracy or culture. Preston-Shoot (2003, p. 12) adds to this with his similar finding that social workers in statutory agencies felt 'internalized oppression,' that is, workers felt that any attempted action to relieve the hardship of services users' lives was futile, so why should they continue to try? Preston-Shoot considered this to be a 'resigned acceptance' (*ibid.*). Such is the strength of this self-definition of powerlessness, that even if workers reflexively identify that they do have power (and Fook, 2012, suggests this might come with experience), they keep it to themselves in order to be accepted by colleagues. In effect, then, if this is applied to a specific context such as a meeting, where a social worker may feel marginalized, for all of the reasons already explored, it can easily be seen that the difficulty in making a contribution or helping service users to do so, might well be exacerbated.

How can reflection help a social worker in a meeting deal with this? Firstly, Fook (2012) identifies that the power social workers are referring to in terms of powerlessness, is formal, structural and hierarchical power. As critical reflection is centrally concerned with upsetting these traditional notions of power (see Chapter 2), social workers must be aware of the other types of power that can be exercised, and use this knowledge in order to empower themselves and service users. From this starting point of deconstructing the power structures within a meeting, the social worker must then create a reconstruction, wherein different types of knowledge are equally valued, where different perspectives are attended to and where the expertise arising from lived experience is highly regarded (Fook, 2012). So, a social worker in a meeting might be able to introduce alternative discourses such as 'Maybe we can hear X's view on that idea...?' or 'As X's social worker, I would like to know...'

As already mentioned, Calder (2003) gives the chairperson of any meeting the overarching responsibility of ensuring that all opinions are heard and all attendees are allowed to contribute. However, Calder does not, perhaps, recognize that the traditional power structures may hinder this to such a degree that explicit awareness and consequent critical action is required to facilitate real participation. Thinking about the case study, it might be that Susan develops a critical awareness of the power dynamics within the meeting, is able to reconstruct the hierarchy of knowledge within a postmodern framework, and can use this to make sure Elsie's view is highly valued. Susan might well introduce a discourse which is uncomfortable for the meeting to hear, and may challenge the groupthink, but which is essential for the empowerment of Elsie. Of course, Susan's ability to do this is fundamentally affected by the quality of her relationship with Elsie. Does she know Elsie well enough to really understand what she thinks and wants, and to empathize with how she might feel about the discussion of her options? Munro (2011) puts the relationship between worker and service user at the heart of social work and, in the current case study, the importance of the relationship is, indeed, obvious.

Reflective Activity 7.3

Look again at the sketch you made for Reflective Activity 7.2. This time, identify where you think the power lay.

1. Are you identifying a traditional hierarchy of power?
2. Can you link this to notions of 'expert' knowledge identified in the previous exercise?
3. Try to deconstruct this, and reconstruct an alternative view.
4. Discuss with your colleague how you might have contributed more to the alternative construction.

Strategies in meetings

As well as developing a critical understanding of the power dynamics and issues of status and group influences upon which they are required to reflect-in-action within meetings, social workers also need to understand some of the strategies that participants in meetings may use for various purposes. Additionally, they need to understand reflexively how they themselves might adopt defensive or other strategies. Some of those strategies will now be discussed.

Noonan (2007) suggests that defensive strategies arise from the potential for embarrassment, from perceived threats or from differences in views. He describes embarrassment not as an over-concern with what others think of us, but rather the feeling caused when others witness or hear something we would rather they had not. In consideration of the Caleb Ness case (O'Brien, 2003), it may be that the nurse could not speak out as strongly as she would have liked to for fear of embarrassment. Would she be able to talk in an evidence-based way about her fears and doubts for Caleb's safety, or was she relying on practice wisdom and gut instinct to inform her opinions? If the basis of her argument consisted of the latter types of knowledge, which might well be undervalued, might she have found it potentially embarrassing to insist that the meeting give due regard to her views? Likewise, might Susan feel that there is potential embarrassment in insisting that Elsie's view be prioritized? Would she look silly to go on about that, in the face of expert medical opinion and evidence-based practice in relation to Elsie's condition? Thinking about this reflexively, with awareness of all of the issues and of how she is feeling, Susan might be able to draw some confidence from the explicit recognition of her values and her duty in relation to making sure Elsie's voice is heard. Reflecting-for-action prior to the meeting, and anticipating that a groupthink might emerge in relation to Elsie going into residential care, Susan might well imagine how she would feel if she does not speak up for fear of embarrassment, and might be able to pre-empt the disjuncture she would cause herself by practising in a way which was so at odds with her value base. As stated in Chapter 1, social workers will go to some lengths to avoid the feeling of disjuncture, such is its corrosive power, so understanding it as a consequence and wanting to avoid it, might be a useful tool in finding the confidence and courage to speak out.

Noonan (2007, p. 44) also talks about threats as triggers for defensive strategies: a threat being defined as something which 'threatens our sense of competency.' When our sense of competency is intact, we feel good because others acknowledge it, or because we feel the satisfaction of a job well done. Noonan describes a typical threat example where another person makes a negative evaluation of an aspect of our work. We either agree that it is true and fair, in which case we will experience embarrassment, or we feel it is unwarranted and unfair, in which case we react to the negative perception of ourself which is at odds with our self perception, and take a defensive position.

Difference in views can also cause defensive strategies to come to the fore, especially if the situation is perceived by the participants as having only a win/lose outcome. The more a person feels their thinking is clear, and that they are right, the higher the stakes in regard to 'winning' the argument. Noonan suggests that differences in views do not necessarily trigger threats or embarrassment and consequent defensiveness, but they can do so. An additional consideration might be that 'losing' a debate in a public forum such as a meeting is more likely to cause embarrassment and threat than doing so in the context of a private debate, so once again, the particular context of a meeting can heighten the emotions involved and can make defensiveness far more likely.

Gambrill (2012) also suggests that people have goals in meetings which do not contribute to sound decision making – showing how bright one is, impressing those with perceived higher status, and disguising one's own lack knowledge of what one is doing. Clearly, Noonan and Gambrill's analyses are very apposite and highlight the importance of these powerful processes.

The potential, then, for embarrassment, threat and differences of opinion, and participants' desire to achieve personal goals, can trigger several defensive strategies. The kinds of strategies which meeting participants might employ include getting locked into head-to-head arguments where neither party listens to the other, emotions are heightened and winning is the only goal; staying silent in order to remain 'safe' from potential threats; physically leaving the meeting under some pretence; making large-scale assumptions by blaming whole classes of people such as 'management,' 'the social work department' or 'social services,' 'the hospital' or 'home care'; and avoiding actually addressing the issues because of social politeness or, as Gambrill suggests, the personal goal of 'appearing normal' (p. 488).

According to Goleman (1995) these defensive responses to perceived threats and fears arise from a basic human instinct for

Reflective Activity 7.4

1. Think reflexively about your own performance within meetings.
2. Reflect on any defensive strategies you adopt within meetings. Why do you use them? What are the purposes? Try to reflect consciously about ways you tend to behave.

survival. Humans can experience theses triggers and the emotional reactions to them, almost unconsciously, as they are derived from our ancient 'flight or fight' mechanism. It is easy, therefore, to see why defensive strategies can perpetuate and go unrecognized for much of the time. In this context, reflexivity is crucial. Explicitly understanding what is causing the trigger and understanding our own reaction to it is of critical importance if potential defensive behaviour is to be avoided.

Conclusion

In terms of relationship-based social work, the families in Ghaffar et al.'s (2012) study of parental experiences in the child protection system valued the relationship with the social worker. They wanted social workers who 'listened to their point of view and who were respectful, honest and consistent' (p. 902), which is congruent with Munro's (2011) promotion of relationship-based social work. In terms of meetings, the powerful influences of dynamics, status and other features as already discussed, can create an extremely difficult environment in which service users are expected to contribute to discussions and decisions. It is, therefore, imperative that the social worker knows the service user's view of the situation and understands what they want to happen, and what they would like to say. This can only be achieved by really getting to know the service user and having a proper professional relationship with them. Once a social worker has established a relationship, and if they are able to critically reflect upon the meeting as above, then they should be able to challenge hierarchical power structures and hopefully help the service user to play a real part in the meeting.

The emotional content of meetings has been explored in terms of feelings about status, hierarchy and power, and also, very importantly, in terms of trigger events and resultant defensive strategies. Arguably, this feature of human behaviour is more acute within a public forum such as a meeting because the trigger events (embarrassment and threat) can be exacerbated. Embarrassment, or negative opinions of our competence, can feel far worse when exposed to an onlooking group of our peers. Liu and Maitlis (2013) conducted a study looking at the role of emotion in relation to strategies adopted by a group meeting within a large business organization. The authors found that positive emotional encounters, characterized by humour, excitement and agreement were associated with 'integrative strategising processes' (Liu and Maitlis, 2013, p. 14) in that meeting members were in agreement and decided on action on that basis. In contrast to this, the researchers found some examples of negative emotional content which were related to different strategies. For example, one encounter involved a team member receiving little feedback or response to his, increasingly excited, appeals for his suggestion to be adopted. This led to frustration on his part and eventual withdrawal. The consequence of this was a fractured strategy, where the member displayed disagreement with other proposals and a general disengagement, which resulted in the postponement of a decision. Another encounter involved two members repeatedly locked into a confrontation which had a significant impact on strategizing, in that too much time was spent on a few proposals, with other promising proposals not given enough time.

In these negative encounters, features of defensive processes can be identified. Withdrawal and silence was displayed by the individual in the first example, perhaps triggered by the lack of positive recognition from the other team members which might have been interpreted as a comment about his competence, and might also have been an embarrassing experience. In the second example, the meeting members seemed to be locked into an imperative to win at all costs. There appeared to be minimal listening to each other and very little hope of, or desire for, compromise or consensus. This can be related to the exacerbating effect of the specific meeting context; to lose might mean an embarrassment or threat, to win might mean recognition and positive confirmation of competence. If a social worker uses any defensive strategy within a meeting it could have deleterious effects on the successful functioning of the meeting and on the social worker's task of supporting and empowering the service user. Defensive strategies are employed, often unconsciously, essentially to protect oneself, and the over-riding concern is to avoid embarrassment or threat. All other objectives, therefore, slip down the priority list. Clearly, then, this would be extremely poor practice and social workers need reflexive awareness in order to avoid it.

In terms of values, a social worker struggling to speak out in a meeting, even after critically deconstructing the dynamics and hierarchy, might reflect upon their values. The British Association of Social Workers (BASW) Code of Ethics states that social workers must respect service users' rights to self determination: 'Social workers should respect, promote and support people's dignity and right to make their own choices and decisions, irrespective of their values and life choices' (BASW, 2011, p. 8). This means that Susan should, ethically, put forward Elsie's view that she wants to go home. This may lead to discussion about risks within which Elsie's view would be accounted for (see Chapter 5 for a further discussion of risk in terms of values). As already mentioned, if Susan were to succumb to the powerful dynamics and influences of the meeting, she might leave feeling very negatively about her own practice. She might experience disjuncture due to the hiatus between her value base and her actions. The very corrosive effects of disjuncture have already been identified and appraised (in Chapter 1) so, as has been shown, we can see that consciously understanding her feelings, and knowing herself as a value-based practitioner, might help Susan act ethically. In essence, it would be up to Susan to understand any reluctance she may feel in speaking out and to undertake a critical analysis of the situation and a reflexive examination of herself, her values and her emotions.

Doel (2006) points out that workers in a group setting such as a meeting might hold different value positions in regards to working practices. He goes on to suggest that these value differences are hidden in one-to-one work with service users but are exposed by the discussion and debate which takes place within a group. He considers this exposure to be a healthy aspect of any group work, and it is important that it is allowed to happen even if service users are present, to demonstrate that there is not one, exact *truth* in social work situations. Once again, this links to the helpfulness of postmodern thinking about power (Fook, 2012).

In conclusion, it is suggested that critical reflection and reflexivity are key to ethical practice within meetings. For example, Gambrill (2012) suggests that the first principle in avoiding groupthink, is that group members be aware of the concept, and aware of its power and consequences. In other words, group members require a reflective understanding of groupthink and a reflexive awareness of their own part in the potential for it to arise.

Furthermore, as Doel (2006) states, power dynamics are accentuated within a meeting and, therefore, the responsibility upon workers to be attuned to them, and to challenge them, is also more acute. Traditional notions of hierarchical power can be very disabling for workers who *perceive* themselves to be of lower status, and to hold less valuable knowledge, *and* for service users who are attempting to take part in the meeting. Social workers must be able to critically analyse all of this and to challenge and offer a reconstruction of the traditional constructs. This significant and complex process is, of course, considerably facilitated by the social worker having a real relationship with the service user.

Further resources

Bissell, G. (2012) *Organizational Behaviour for Social Work.*
For further reading about the wider organizational features of social work.

Doel, M. (2006) *Using Groupwork.*
Will aid understanding and expand the reader's knowledge of group processes and dynamics.

Noonan, W.R. (2007) *Discussing the Undiscussable: A Guide to Overcoming Defensive Routines in the Workplace.*
An excellent text for those who want to read further about defensive strategies at work.

CHAPTER 8

Records and report writing

Written articulation and recording is an important facet of social work. This chapter will explore the role of critical reflection under the following themes:

- The place of writing in social work
- Reflection and writing
- Writing professionalism and relationships

Rashid's Diary (Manager of Young Person's Residential Unit, Key Worker for Robbie)

Monday
Read daily logs from shift staff
10.00–2.00 Support and supervision with care staff
3.00 Unit Team meeting
4.30 Thoughts and reflection on team meeting content
Write daily log for shift staff

Tuesday
Read daily logs from shift staff
2.00 Writing case notes as Key worker (x 5)
Write daily log for shift staff

Wednesday
Read daily logs from shift staff
emails
10.00 Reflection and thought about care plan for Robbie
10.30 Write care plan
Write daily log for shift staff

Thursday
Day off

Friday
Day off

Saturday
Read daily logs from shift staff
10.00 Outing with boys to play football
1.00 Unit Lunch
Write daily log for shift staff

Sunday
Read daily logs from shift staff
10.00 Write formal report about Robbie
Write daily log for shift staff

Case Study 8.1

Rashid is the manager of a residential unit for young people. He combines the administrative and managerial elements of this role with a strong commitment and enthusiasm for continuing to work directly with the young people who reside at the unit. Rashid has been appointed as key worker for a new young person in the unit called Robbie. Robbie is presenting a significant behavioural challenge within the unit and has been involved in a series of violent outbursts that have led to significant damage to the unit's property and has also unsettled the existing group of residents. This is not an uncommon set of circumstances for young people as they adjust to the losses, new relationships and challenges associated with a move into a residential unit, and Rashid knows that he must bear this context in mind when he responds to the presenting behaviours. Robbie has been particularly verbally abusive towards Rashid with regular disparaging comments about Rashid's North African origins.

Rashid is responsible for a range of written recordings relating to Robbie's experience in the residential unit, and these include daily logs (to be passed between staff from shift to shift), detailed case notes, care plans and formal reports. These types of written recording are interlinked in the sense that they are all part of the recorded history of Robbie's experiences and progress within residential care.

The questions below will help reflect on Rashid's feelings and values, as well as reflecting on recording of information.

Reflective Activity 8.1

1. Consider the type of information that might be recorded in each of the types of written recording noted above. Are there any differences? If so, why might that be?
2. Why might it be important for Rashid to engage in critical reflection prior to writing these recordings?
3. Consider the balance in this case between Rashid's professional role and the impact of his personal feelings and values.

The place of writing in social work

It is not unusual to hear social workers bemoaning the amount of paperwork associated with their roles. Written recordings in social work are often pitted against direct practice in such discussions and the balance between the two activities is often a source of consternation. This implicit division between actual practice and the written recording and articulation of it is unhelpful as they are both crucial activities in the daily lives of social workers. Prince (1996) notes that although writing in social work is often seen as a routine, process-driven activity, it is in fact through the written articulation of practice that professional judgement and accountability are most clearly presented. Healy and Mulholland (2012) note that there are many different types of writing in social work. These include reports, case notes, reflective logs, contracts, letters and funding proposals.

This leads to two important characteristics of writing, namely its permanence and its primacy. Much of this book considers case studies, describing and analysing interactions and relationships that social workers have with service users, colleagues and other professionals. The reflective processes in these cases enable reflection prior to, during and after the event (Schön, 1983; Fook and Askeland, 2006). This allows social workers to evaluate the effectiveness of their actions and feed this into future practice and/or clarify or revise behaviours 'within the moment'. Simply put, the actions of social workers are fluid and adaptable. The written articulation of this practice is much less flexible, and once it is 'down in writing', it may be read, used and communicated across a range of forums without further opportunity for change. This is why written recordings take on a significant status in the lexicon of social work communication (Lishman, 2009), and why the need for critical reflection and clarity of decision making in the writing process is overwhelming.

Stanton (2004) notes that writing helps shape culture and influence beliefs and understandings. In the context of social work, this is very evident in the role that the written articulation of practice and its associated recommendations has in shaping decisions affecting the lives of service users (Koprowska, 2005). For the written output of social workers to have the requisite degree of authenticity and validity, its content must be accurate, current and accessible (Lishman, 2009).

It might be useful to briefly consider these facets in relation to the case study. For Rashid to record accurately the content of his work with Robbie, he may need to draw on the following streams of information:

- The views of Robbie
- The relevant policy and legislative context of residential care and social work with young people
- The theoretical and research evidence base that underpins and informs this area of practice

- An awareness of the impact and use of self within the relationship with Robbie.

This list may not be exhaustive, but it does suggest that Rashid will need to take time to step back from his practice and contextualize and reflect upon the *meaning* of his account of practice. We noted that Robbie has personalized his aggression towards Rashid. This is likely to have a personal impact on Rashid and may raise a complex set of emotions, which he has to acknowledge and consider. Rosenberg (1990) talks of the importance of reflexivity and self-knowledge in relation to emotions. If Rashid can engage in a significant degree of reflection about his feelings, then not only may he be able manage the potential negative impact on his view of Robbie, but also be able to use these emotions as a source of *motivation* (Barrett, 2012) to work with Robbie through his transition and *understand* how Robbie may be feeling.

The process of writing the types of recordings noted in the case study will present Rashid with an opportunity to order, edit and prioritize his thinking in relation to his work with Robbie. Moon (2004) notes that the process of writing can be in itself reflective due to the aforementioned stepping back and ordering of thought. In the case of the completion of a daily log, the opportunity for reflection may be limited, but the underpinning professional responsibility is the same in terms of accuracy and accessibility. This clearly requires Rashid to engage in active reflection at the moment of his practice and to seek informal opportunities to examine his practice. For example, Bolton and Boyd (2003) note the importance of 'private spaces' (i.e. supervision) to enable colleagues to step aside from their professional persona (whatever the professional context) and explore the interaction between their own responses and the requirements of the professional role. In this case, Rashid, may be able to locate his personal feelings in the wider context of the practice, and, crucially, not feel they have to be suppressed or ignored.

Healy and Mulholland (2012) point out that case notes are focused and factual accounts of the process and on-going assessment of practice which can be used as an historical record of involvement for the individual worker, colleagues and, potentially, service users. They note that formal reports have a direct impact on decision making forums and processes, and as such need to be accurate, fair and clear. What unites these two types of writing, and

Reflective Activity 8.2

1. How do you feel about the written aspects of your practice? Do you view them as part of the process of your practice and critical reflection, or simply a functional recording?
2. Using the list of sources of information that are suggested above for Rashid as a basis for an example from your practice, start to unpick the key elements relating to your chosen case. Are there any surprising themes emerging?
3. How can the themes that emerge be used as a source of information to underpin your writing?

any other written recordings in social work, is that they are under-pinned by a *professional purpose*.

Healy and Mulholland (2012) suggest that importance of the professional role means that social workers should reflect the codes of practice in terms of the content and focus of their writing. For example, they should seek to acknowledge and value the views and perspectives of service users. This underlines the need for the written recording of practice to be viewed with the same degree of status and importance as any other facet of practice (rather than an additional and time-consuming task). Indeed, Lishman (2009) notes that the permanency of written recordings gives writing an evidential status which can be used in statutory and non-statutory decision making forums, and also are accessible to the service users to which they pertain (Data Protection Act, 1998). This further underlines the need for written recordings to be honest, clear, accurate and up to date.

Reflection and writing

Ingram (2012b) undertook a study of social workers in a UK Local Authority to examine the role of emotions in their practice. A key finding was the lack of opportunity to undertake reflective writing outside of formal education and training. Many social workers responded that they quite simply never write reflectively in the sense of reflecting for its own purpose. This is, of course, not to overlook the reflective elements of producing written recordings of practice. In a sense, all formal writing in social work involves implicit or explicit reflection and thinking about the content of practice. Ingram reported isolated examples of reflective diaries being made for supervision purposes, but this was rare and was reliant on the relationship between supervisor and supervisee. This is mirrored by implicit messages in key social work textbooks relating to writing (see Healy and Mulholland, 2012) where there is no explicit reference to reflective writing.

This suggests that, in regard to the opportunities and requirements to undertake reflective writing, there may be a chasm between social work education and frontline practice. It is common for social work students to be required to write reflective accounts during and at the end of all practice learning opportunities and to prepare for supervision sessions by maintaining a reflective journal. Students are required to do this because of the belief that it is important for them to think about their practice in a critical and analytical manner and record this accordingly. They are encouraged to consider their emotional reactions and values alongside identifying other sources which impact upon what they do and why they do it. Through this process, a student is then able to demonstrate a deeper understanding of their practice and their development as a social worker. Ward (2010) notes the importance of education and practice having strong links and synergies; failure to implement the keeping of reflective journals seems to be a stark example of pressures of resources and time, when coupled with an outcome-focused conception of supervision and practice, driving a wedge between education and practice. Encouragingly, Ward (2010) and Moon (2004) suggest that an audience is not required for reflective writing to be useful. It is the process of ordering, editing and thinking associated with reflective writing that is the key. This chimes with the suggestion by Hafford-Letchfield (2009) that learning cultures inside social work organizations can be *informal and self-led* as well as more formally structured.

It would be hard to argue against the usefulness of reflection and its written form, yet it appears to be marginalized owing to competing pressures and approaches. Hennessey (2011) and Howe (2008) both note the importance of being able to step away from one's practice and have space to express and explore the complex and confusing elements of practice. Whether this is undertaken in writing or in other forums such as supervision, it is clear that a cultural ethos needs to be developed which encourages and values it. If such a cultural shift is made, then a context of trust and safety may be developed to support it. Heron and Murray (2004) note

Reflective Activity 8.3

1. Do you have the opportunity to write reflective logs relating to your practice? If not, how might you facilitate its inclusion in the culture of your organization?
2. Identify the reflective aspects of your approach to formal case notes and reports? Do you reflect upon your emotions and values in the process? If so, do they then contribute to your written recordings?

that there appears to be a division between the written world of academia and that of practice. They suggest that social work needs to adopt a *'writing identity'* to culturally facilitate the place of writing (both reflective and academic) in the context of social work practice (*ibid.*, p. 203). This sits comfortably with the ethos of continuing professional development and as such may culturally and organizationally be a necessity rather than an aspiration.

Given the preceding discussion about the permanency of writing, it may be that the complex, personal and uncertain elements of reflections on practice may look rather exposed when written down. An opportunity for Rashid would be to find an audience for his written reflections. This takes us back to the issue of organizational and professional culture. The increased emphasis on post-registration training may provide a potential opportunity to engage in reflective writing. This section has underlined the reflective elements of writing in social work, but has also highlighted that explicit reflective writing exercises may be marginalized due to competing pressures and organizational cultures. It is to the theme of professional culture and identity that this chapter will now turn.

Writing, professionalism and relationships

A core theme of this book is the importance of the 'softer' elements of social work practice such as emotions and values to be viewed as significant aspects of the construct of the social work professional. Ingram (2012b) found that the overwhelming majority of social workers surveyed stated that they did not write about the emotional aspects of their practice in written recordings. This was often linked to the notion of needing to 'be professional' (see also Chapter 2), despite a similarly overwhelming view that emotions were a core aspect of practice (Munro, 2011). This is an important message for a book such as this, as it suggests that the centrality of reflection noted elsewhere may be edited, omitted and marginalized in the context of professional writing. The notion of being a professional is often underpinned by technical-rational constructs, where certainty and tangible outcomes are of high value (Brodie, Nottingham and Plunkett, 2008). When professionalism is viewed through this lens then it is more easily understood why the 'harder' and more tangible elements of social work practice are predominantly recorded.

It is worth returning to the idea proposed by Healy and Mulholland (2012) – that the written recording of social work is underpinned by the codes of practice. They note in conjunction with this point that case notes and reports need to be factual and accurate. Taking this link to professional codes and values a step further; it is useful to pick up on the use of the words 'factual' and 'accurate'. It was clear from Ingram (2012b) that such qualities were seen as an obstacle and deterrent in terms of writing about emotions. It seemed that accuracy and validity were linked to outcomes of processes and tangible certainties. Contemplating the discussion earlier in this chapter about the importance of critically reflecting upon the complexities and challenges within practice, then it seems that to remove these aspects of practice from written recording, or even to edit them down, will result in the presentation of a less than 'accurate' or 'factual' account. This could turn the view of the construct of 'being professional' on its head, in the sense that that to write an account of practice that is authentic and seeks to present the process and content of practice in an open and genuine fashion *must* involve discussion of emotions, values and the relationship between the social worker and service user. This chimes with Munro (2011) who argues that these aspects of practice should be viewed as a source of information (alongside other streams of information and knowledge) that is useful and credible. They are, of course, to be placed within the context of legislation, theory and policy.

However, the *professional purpose* of writing in social work provides the current discussion with enough leverage to stake a claim for challenging the marginalization of the interpersonal/relationship based elements of social work in written recordings. Healy and Mulholland (2012, p. 87) suggest that it is 'essential to cite the sources of professional opinion' in writing. It could be suggested that if social workers are to present their practice in a transparent and accurate manner and be able to represent the nature, content and dynamics of the relationship at the heart of the practice, then emotions and values are one of the key sources of their professional judgement. If this centrality of relationships in social work is accepted, then emotions and values would seem to be a key defining feature of the profession, and of associated judgements and opinions. It is, of course, essential that social workers make clear the nature of the content of their writing, whether it is factual, opinion or feeling, but having done so they should be comfortable in the knowledge that they are presenting the richness and depth of their practice. This depth would improve the usability and communicability of written records and reports, which would fit with the messages of Munro (2011) in terms of the importance of relationships with service users.

Rashid's practice will take place within the competing professional paradigms discussed above. The case study highlights the potential personal impact of Robbie's behaviour on Rashid, but also notes the professional commitment and knowledge that Rashid has in his work supporting young people in residential care settings. When Rashid is undertaking critical reflection for the purposes of producing case notes or reports, he will be able to contextualize the presenting issues. For example, he will be able to draw upon his theoretical knowledge of attachment theory and loss to understand the impact on Robbie of reception into residential care. He will also be able to recognize the dissonance between his professional commitment to support Robbie and his personal feelings regarding the verbal abuse he has received. These reflections may allow Rashid to strive to establish a relationship based on trust and respect underpinned by his professional codes (GSCC, 2010) and personal motivations. When these strands of reflection are considered together, Rashid may be able to record recommendations regarding the future support of Robbie which recognize the potential impact of his behaviours on workers and peers and in turn locate these within the 'harder' streams of information such as legislation and theory. If the rational-technical presentation of practice is applied instead, Rashid may edit out the complexities of his developing relationship with Robbie and in turn reduce the depth of the assessment. This version of the process may result in the same recommendations about how to support Robbie, but will not allow the process of reaching these recommendations to be fully communicated, and in turn colleagues and future workers may enter their work with Robbie under-informed about what has gone before.

Reflective Activity 8.4

Choose a piece of practice that you are currently involved with, and then consider and write about the following aspects of it:

1. What theory and knowledge can you identify which helps explain what is happening and can help to predict future actions and decisions that you might make?
2. What are your emotional reactions to the service user involved in this practice and where do you think they come from?
3. Consider whether you can use both these elements in your formal writing about the case. What are the challenges of this and what does this say about your view of 'being professional'?

There is also, of course, a potential usefulness in Robbie being able to read and maintain a record of his experiences of residential care to help him better understand his strengths and the impact of some of his behaviour on others. If this is edited out then this usefulness may be reduced or removed. Similarly, if it is accepted that openness and genuineness are key characteristics of what service users wish to find in their social workers (Harding and Beresford, 1995), then there is an argument for the fruits of critical reflection feeding into the communications with service users. Hopkins (1998) notes that for this to be effective, social workers must ensure that they write in a manner which is accessible and jargon-free. It is of course important to note that the purpose and focus of professional writing cannot be disregarded, and that the material written down must meet the requirements of accuracy, validity and clarity. Where this is not evident or achievable, then clearly those aspects of reflection remain in the private sphere of the worker. For example, Rashid may share that Robbie's behaviour had an impact on him, but should not use a written report to vent his anger. This further underlines the benefit of deep critical reflection as part of the preparation for writing.

Conclusion

A great deal has been said throughout this chapter that relates to the Reflective Social Work Practitioner Model proposed in Chapter 1. In a sense, this chapter may well be viewed as the one where the model is most vulnerable or at least compromised. This is due to the aforementioned emphasis on the rational-technical recording of practice (Healy and Mulholland, 2012: Ingram, 2012b). When one adopts this approach to the recording of practice, relationship-based aspects can be squeezed out to make space for evidence-based outcomes and recommendations. In a sense, report writing (and, to a lesser extent, case notes) can become less about the process of reaching decisions and recommendations, and more about evidencing and defending those decisions.

This does not sit comfortably with our model, as it is recognized that practice and the reflections associated with it will include the concrete knowledge aspects noted above *and* the experiences and dynamics involved in the relationships at the heart of practice. It is heartening that national narratives of the profession counter the limited construct of the profession evident in written recording (Scottish Government, 2006; Department of Children, Schools and Families, 2009; Munro, 2011). It is important to note that despite the challenges to the model posed in this chapter, it is not the case that critical reflection does not take place, or does not inform the written aspects of practice. Rather, it is subsequent editing of the presentation of such reflections that may take place. The example of Rashid illustrated that reflections on the interpersonal aspects of a piece of practice may not only be interesting but also *useful* in terms of recommendations and subsequent actions.

It has been noted that the editing, analysing and prioritizing that contribute to the process of putting information into written form is inextricably linked to processes of reflection and reflexivity. In this sense, the written recording of practice creates a forum and opportunity for social workers to engage in critical reflection. It was further remarked that the fruits of a social worker's reflections may be edited prior to writing in formal case notes and reports. It is at this juncture that the authors identified a challenge to the reflective practitioner model, and potential opportunities for broadening the scope and content of writing in social work.

Further resources

Heron, G. and Murray, R. (2004) 'The place of writing in social work', *Journal of Social Work*, 4(2), 199–214.
   Explores the role that writing, and particularly academic writing has in social work.

Hopkins, G. (1998) *Plain English for social services.*
Excellent examples of writing to support practitioners to write in a clear and accessible manner.

Moon, J. (1999) *Reflection in learning and professional development.*
Makes a strong case for the use of reflection for practitioners and students alike.

CHAPTER 9

Effective supervision: reflection, support and direction

This chapter explores the opportunities that social workers may have to engage in critical reflection within the organizations in which they work. Supervision is a key source of support and guidance for social workers, and this chapter will examine the challenges and opportunities inherent in this relationship and consider ways in which workers can navigate their way through such a variable landscape. The following topics will feature in this chapter:

- The role of supervision
- Differing constructs of supervision
- Informal peer support
- The role of organizational culture

Sandra's diary (Social worker based in a local authority, dealing with young offenders)

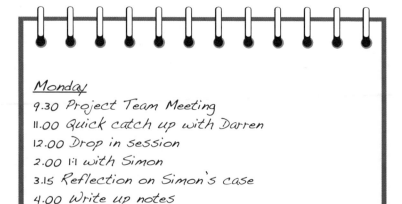

Monday
9.30 Project Team Meeting
11.00 Quick catch up with Darren
12.00 Drop in session
2.00 1:1 with Simon
3.15 Reflection on Simon's case
4.00 Write up notes

Tuesday
10.00 _Group work session with eight young people_
12.00 _Drop-in session_
1.00 _Lunch with Colin at El Aperitivo (discuss D and S)_
2.30 _Activity session at local sports centre_

Wednesday
9.30 1:1 _with Darren_
10.30 _Girls' group_
4.30 _Make notes for support and supervision (note* Simon's attitude)_
7.30 _Drop in Session: Planning car maintenance project_

Thursday
9.30 _Support and supervision_
12.00 _Reflection on support and supervision_
2.00 _Check plans for residential on Saturday._
3.00 _Phone parents to remind about trip_
4.00 _confirm minibus driver_
4:30 1:1 _with Darren_

Friday
Day off

Saturday
Residential trip - rock climbing

Sunday

Case Study 9.1

Sandra is a social worker based in a local authority project with young offenders. She has recently begun working on a one-to-one basis with Darren to look at his offending behaviour. Sandra has a caseload of 18 young people whom she works with individually and in group-work contexts.

She has found working with Darren enjoyable as he is a very engaging and open young person. She has found herself thinking about Darren's case in the evenings and often worries about him during the weekend in case he offends again. She has undertaken a degree of reflection and recognizes that part of her heightened interest in Darren's case is that he reminds her of her younger brother in a positive way. This has made her feel that she can tune into Darren's situation more easily and it contributes to her feelings of concern and protectiveness. Sandra has managed to meet with Darren with greater frequency than she would normally (three times per week instead of once) and is highly motivated to seek the best resources available to her to help intervene.

The other key case that is presenting her with a challenge is her work with Simon, an 18 year old who has been convicted of sexual offences against younger children. Her work with Simon is at an early stage, and she is finding it difficult to manage her feelings of anger and resentment in relation to his non-cooperation and apparent refusal to take any responsibility for his offences. These feelings are making it difficult for her to step back from the case and establish a positive way forward.

The questions in Reflective Activity 9.1 will help the reader consider the importance of reflection for Sandra and forums available to her and themselves to reflect.

Reflective Activity 9.1

1. How might reflection help Sandra identify the best course of action in these cases? For example, why does she feel motivated in the first case but cannot manage her negative feelings in the second case? Why are emotions important in professional practice?
2. Which forums, do you think, are available to Sandra to reflect and explore the complexities of these two cases?
3. If you had similar cases, what forum would you have to reflect and explore such complexities?
4. What might be the problems and challenges for Sandra when exploring the ethical and emotional dimensions of these cases?

As can be seen, social workers juggle a range of case responsibilities, and at any given time there are likely to be an ever changing array of challenges, dilemmas and opportunities that arise within such workloads. In the example above, we are presented with two issues that are at the forefront of Sandra's mind as she enters her working week. The cases present her with different challenges at an individual level in terms of her emotional reactions. They also need to be thought about and located contextually across a range of domains including policy, organizational culture, wider workloads, professional codes and personal resources. Therefore, it is important to consider where Sandra can best articulate, explore and reflect upon her practice.

The role of supervision

The answer to the question of where social workers may find the space and conditions for reflection is likely to include reference to the role of supervision. Supervision is most commonly constructed to be a protected session between a social worker and a senior colleague; one which brings together individual and wider organizational interests (Keen et al., 2009). This union requires the supervisor and supervisee to manage and balance a range of competing demands and agendas. For example, Beddoe (2010) considers the competing demands for workers to be allowed space to explore the uncertainties of practice and the technical activity of following the indicators and procedures associated with risk management. The key tension for Beddoe, and one which is evident across a range of literature (Smith, 2000; Department of Children, Schools and Families, 2009; Hafford-Letchfield, 2009; Munro, 2011), is related to the multiplicity of functions of supervision and the participants within it. Simply put, the opportunity for finding the space, time and culture to facilitate reflection in supervision can be counterbalanced by managerial functions which may focus on economy, efficiency and effectiveness (Gorman, 2000). These tensions can often seem unreconcilable. However, if it is accepted that the experience of social work practice contains blurry complex issues (Schon, 1983), and that the relationship-based aspects of practice necessitate the social worker engaging in genuine and open 'human level' interactions, then it is possible to see that any supervision relationship that purports to examine social work practice, must have space to allow workers to consider their use of self and the implications of their values and beliefs upon their practice (Hennessey, 2011; Ingram, 2012a).

There are many variations in terms of possible models of supervision. However, the one proposed by Kadushin (1976) picks up on the key recurrent themes. Kadushin proposes that supervision should have a managerial, supportive and educational function. It is clear that reflection can sit very comfortably in relation to support and education in terms of seeking depth and clarity in a worker's practice. To reduce the perceived disjuncture between those themes and the management function of supervision, it could be argued that reflection must allow social workers to think about their practice in terms of wider contextual and organizational factors. By pulling that aspect of reflection into supervision, it is possible to unify the strands and create a potentially reflective forum for social workers. Bogo and McKnight (2006) note that even when one views supervision as a tool to simply ensure that the agency's service is delivered well and efficiently, reflection and support are central to achieving such performance.

Schreiber and Frank (1983) highlight the role of peer support through the use of a group supervision approach. This takes supervision and support away from the familiar one-to-one model described above and instead values and utilizes the knowledge that is held within teams of social workers. They found that social workers valued the opportunity to share knowledge and experiences with peers who were involved with similar professional challenges. This model of supervision could be seen to emphasize the educational and supportive element proposed by Kadushin (1976) but makes the managerial elements less clear and present. Kadushin and Harkness (2002) note that group supervision may ameliorate the potential inhibiting aspects of the power dynamics contained within the agency/management functions of supervision noted above, due to the centrality of the 'supervisor' being dispersed across a group. They note that such an approach to supervision is potentially attractive to organizations as there are efficiencies in time and source to be gained by providing supervision simultaneously to staff in a group context.

Supervision could present Sandra with a crucial reflective forum to explore the challenges relating to her work with Darren. A key aspect of this case is her personal attunement with Darren. It seems that this has had a profound impact on her motivation to seek resources for him. On the face of it, this may seem a positive and easily presented case for Sandra within supervision. However, the issue of identification and attunement requires unpicking as it may lead to collusion, assumptions and lack of criticality if left unexplored, and therefore she would benefit from the support of a supervisor. In terms of the management function of supervision, it is clear that there may be implications for the efficient use of resources relating to the additional meetings she schedules with Darren and also the wider impact on other cases she is involved with (if unchecked, there is a danger that a two-tier service where service users we positively identify with are given priority). This is where the reflection in supervision can forge links between the personal and the organizational, and in turn establish the connections rather than the differences.

Sandra's involvement with Simon provides a useful counterpoint. Her feelings of anger and resentment about Simon's presentation may potentially have a crucial impact on her actions. This chimes with Ferguson (2005) who vividly described the impact of suppressed emotions in relation to the Victoria Climbie case in terms of the actions (and inaction) of workers involved. Given the space to reflect upon her feelings, and how and where these may come from, Sandra may be able to stand back from her practice and locate her feelings, and, indeed, Simon, within a clearer context. For example, Sandra should be encouraged to consider why Simon may be uncooperative towards her (and possibly social workers in general). By doing so, Simon's behaviour may become explicable, and in turn may open the door for considering alternative approaches, such as motivational interviewing, to engage with Simon .This example is important, as it seeks to establish a link between reflection, understanding of one's own emotions and those

Reflective Activity 9.2

1. Have you been able to discuss your emotions in a workplace setting? If yes, who was that with? Why did you choose them to discuss your emotions with?
2. What skills and qualities would a supervisor possess to be able to facilitate reflection on emotions?
3. Do you think that emotions and the workplace sometimes clash? Why?
4. From your experience, to what extent would you share these elements of your practice and emotions with your supervisor? Why is that?

of others, and subsequent action and application of knowledge. This clearly echoes the central tenets of emotional intelligence discussed in Chapter 1 in terms of emotional awareness, regulation and attunement (Goleman, 1995; Ingram, 2013).

A collaborative approach to reflective supervision

The preceding discussion provides a useful introduction to the role of supervision in providing opportunities for reflection. The potential challenges posed by contextual factors such as limited time and managerialist conceptions of supervision might suggest social workers are simply at the mercy of their context and the quality of supervision on offer. This need only be part of the picture. If it is accepted that the notion of a reflective organization (Morrison, 2007) is desirable, then the challenge is to consider how to establish the conditions required to make it a reality.

Jindal-Snape and Ingram (2013) developed a model of supervision (SuReCom model) which sought to encourage and facilitate a partnership approach to supervision, one that allowed both parties to clarify the balance and nature of the expected supervision relationship and in turn adjust and modify it accordingly. If this SuReCom model is taken as a starting point and is developed further in the context of reflective social work supervision, it can lay the foundations for a co-created vision of supervision (see Figure 9.1).

This model is useful as a visual illustration of where the balance of supervision can be plotted and also as a *tool* for constructing and reviewing the place of reflection in supervision. This dual function of the model is crucial in terms of its application as it acknowledges the dynamic and fluid nature of supervisory relationships. The model allows the supervisor and supervisee to plot their desired vision of supervision at any point on both axes. One can plot the degree to which a facet of supervision is relevant at any point on both axes. This is likely to move the discussion through the following stages (Ingram, 2012b, p.11):

- **Aspiration** – the use of this model would allow for each party to plot where they would hope the balance of supervision would lie.
- **Negotiation** – having plotted the aspirational balance, any divergence in view can be explored and discussed.

- **Agreement** – the model can then be used to reach an agreed balance, which can be linked to organizational and national perspectives.
- **Review** – the model can be revisited at any stage to consider whether the agreement is still valid or is requiring adjustment.

As can be seen in Figure 9.1, quadrant A depicts a supervisory relationship which emphasizes critical reflection but with less of a focus on practical casework issues. Quadrant B represents a balance between the reflective and practical elements of casework and would reflect a supervisory relationship where both elements are seen as valid and appropriate. Quadrant C depicts a supervisory relationship where the practical elements of casework take centre stage at the expense of critical reflection. Finally, quadrant D shows a supervisory relationship which neither focuses on the practical, nor the reflective aspects of practice. It is difficult to envisage such a supervisory approach as it sidesteps both the aforementioned constructs of supervision.

Figure 9.2 shows how the expectations of each participant in the supervisory relationship can map their views against the other. This

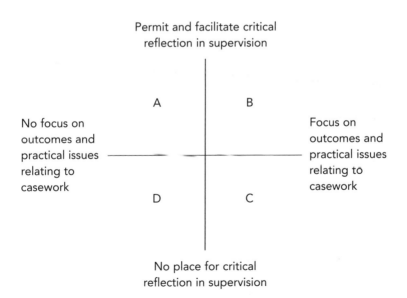

Figure 9.1 Supervision: focus on outcomes and critical reflection.
Source: adapted from Jindal-Snape and Ingram (2013)

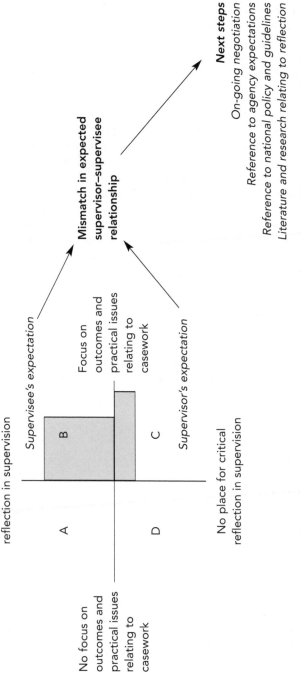

Figure 9.2 An example of a mismatch in expectations between supervisor and supervisee. *Source:* adapted from Jindal-Snape and Ingram (2013)

in turn may allow for clarity about any tensions or divergence in expectations.

It is clear from Figure 9.2, that the supervisee seeks opportunities to engage in critical reflection alongside the practical elements of their caseload, whilst the supervisor favours a practical focus. What is also useful about this model is the flexibility allowed in terms of plotting at any point on an axis to indicate the intensity anticipated. Should there be a mismatch, a guide to potential sources of advice and support have been included under 'next steps' which are intended to serve help protect the place of critical reflection in supervision and avoid the potentially damaging effects this can have on workers and practice (Ferguson, 2005). For example, both parties could look to professional codes to underpin their discussions. This would help to serve as a reminder of the centrality of fostering positive relationships with service users and the professional accountability associated with maintaining trust and respect within these relationships (GSCC, 2002).

In relation to the case study, the use of such an approach would safeguard against Sandra's emotional responses to Simon and Darren remaining unexplored. In relation to Simon, this will give an opportunity to unpick her feelings of anger and irritation, and feelings of protection for Darren. It will provide her the opportunity to be reflexive and consider what her value base is and what the triggers are for her emotional response (see Chapter 1 for discussion of values, emotions and Chapter 2 for reflexivity). It is also important for Sandra to be able to consider Darren within the wider social and structural spheres, in order to consider the impact of issues such as social exclusion on Darren. Where this does not happen, either Sandra or her supervisor can return to the agreed balance of supervision as a vehicle for cementing the need for reflection and minimizing the possibility for 'routinized' practice and emotional suppression.

Reflective Activity 9.3

1. If you were to plot your aspirations for reflective supervision in accordance with Figure 9.1, where would the balance lie? Why is that?
2. How would you feel about negotiating the balance with your supervisor? Why is that?
3. What sources of support might you use to reinforce your claim for desired opportunities for reflection in supervision?

Out-sourced modes of supervision

The discussion so far has largely considered supervision within the familiar paradigm of a senior colleague in the team being responsible for its provision. This led to the consideration of the challenges that the conflation of managerial responsibilities and the therapeutic aspects of supervision may give rise to. Beddoe (2010) notes the emergence of out-sourced supervision arrangements in New Zealand, in which social workers receive supervision from outwith the agency either in addition to or instead of more familiar in-house arrangements. Gibelman and Schervish (1997) look to the model of clinical supervision as a useful framework in terms of placing a key focus on the interpersonal dynamics of the social worker's practice and the relationships contained within it. This, they argue, requires the organizational functions to be less central to the content of supervision. This is in part to facilitate the critically reflective 'space' that can be squeezed into the aforementioned managerially flavoured supervision. The key argument for such arrangements is the potential for a safer environment in which the complex and uncertain elements of practice can be explored without being subject to the pressures of time and potential line-management-related appraisal. This was echoed by the social workers interviewed by Ingram (2012b), who reported that the issue of 'safety' was crucial when considering the ability to engage in reflective supervision. A key contention was that to explore uncertainties in practice could be conflated with 'not coping' or poor practice. In the context of the case study such messages regarding safety would have a significant impact on what Sandra felt able to explore and share. Beddoe (2010, p. 1292) sums up this tension when she states that 'social work hovers in the uncomfortable places, always caught between transformative aspirations and bureaucratic constraints'.

There are, of course, limitations to the outsourcing approach. Perhaps the simplest question to raise would be the extent to which such arrangements undermine the aspiration that critical reflection should be an integral part of the core of learning organizations (SCIE, 2004). There is a danger that it suggests that critical reflection is not the business of social work agencies and that it sits at arm's length from the work of the agency. Perhaps most concerning would be the potential for critical reflection to happen in one arena and then not be transferable or communicable back into the agency or indeed the practice. Additionally, it is crucial for supervision and any associated reflective processes to have an impact on practice and consequently have clear transparent lines of accountability and responsibility. This becomes blurred when there are out-sourced and/or multiple supervisory environments. Ingram (2012b) found that out-sourced supervisory arrangements are often offered in the spirit of a health and welfare provision (akin perhaps to counselling). Such arrangements may contain a reflective function but again risk an unhelpful division between reflection and organizational culture. Returning to the notion of the learning organization, it is instructive to note that a core element of this is the need for learning to involve all people across all domains *within* an organization and that there is a willingness to explore new ideas and foster debate and reflection (Senge, 1990).

It is useful to consider the seminal work of Hochschild (1983) in relation to the impact of organizational culture on the behaviour of employees. Hochschild was interested in how flight attendants managed the organizational requirement to smile and present oneself in a positive manner regardless of one's own feelings. The key argument being that organizational culture can play a significant part in how workers *act* and the permissions they feel they have regarding behaviours. In the context of social work it is possible to consider this Hochschild in the context of supervision. If there explicit and encouraging organizational messages about the role of reflection within supervision, then social workers will feel permitted to engage with reflection. This may also reduce the potential disjuncture between the relationship based aspects of practice and the rational-technical aspects (see Chapter 1).

Informal support network and reflection

It is clear from the diary entries of Sandra, that she has structured office-based time and informal contact with a valued colleague Colin. In addition to this, it is important to consider the place of reflection within the multifarious informal opportunities for reflection and support which present themselves within the offices, corridors and staff rooms of social work agencies. Ingram (2012b) found that informal contact with colleagues was seen by social workers as the most commonly used support and opportunity for reflection within the studied local authority. This is a stark message about the place that more visible forums such as supervision may have in the hierarchy of reflective forums. This sits comfortably with the notion of learning organizations in its broadest sense, as it chimes with associated characteristics such as teamwork, shared beliefs and collaboration (SCIE, 2004). Thomas and Spreadbury (2008) highlight the role of *communities of practice* which reflect the coming together of social workers to share ideas and issues in forums less formal than supervision. Ingram (2012b) found that there were a range of factors which made informal reflection and support very attractive, and these can usefully be mapped against the case study.

- **Shared expertise** – Sandra may value meeting her colleague Colin for lunch to discuss practice situations as he may have similar experiences and can 'tune in' to the circumstances and share practice wisdom. This shared experience sets a balanced foundation for engaging in critical reflection, with the ability to explore uncertain and unsettling issues (such as her anger about Simon) in depth; comparative examples can be used to support this.
- **Unrecorded** – informal contact with colleagues is by its very nature an unrecorded activity in its most common form. This helps to counteract the issues of 'safety' required for meaningful reflection. This would allow Sandra to explore the complexities of her cases without feeling the pressure to attain immediate clarity or to be seen to be 'doing the right thing' straight away. Simply put, the unrecorded nature of such contacts lends greater freedom to test out hypotheses and ideas without risking formally recorded judgements of such ruminations.
- **Accessible** – This type of support is often available 'on the spot' and can allow workers to step back from their practice and reflect at points when it is most acutely required or to allow reflection to be integrated into the ongoing activities relating to a case rather than waiting for the structured supervisor, by which point significant actions may have been taken without reflection.
- **Preparation** – This would allow Sandra to explore issues prior to a more formal presentation of her practice in forums such as supervision or case notes. This, in a sense, allows Sandra to do some of the 'reflective groundwork' to allow more focused reflection within the time constraints of formal supervision. This may help to maintain the place of reflection in supervision and also reflect a desirable reflective culture within organizations.

The availability of informal reflective support from colleagues and peers is not without its potential pitfalls and frailties. These can be summed up as follows:

- **Availability** – by its very nature, the unstructured and informal aspects of colleague support are vulnerable to inconsistent supply and availability. The availability may affected by team size, quality of relationships with colleagues, limited resources and physical space.
- **Quality** – the attractiveness of reflecting upon one's practice with colleagues who have experienced similar practice challenges is attractive. However, the quality of the process and content of such interactions is less easily quality assured and may involve competing agendas and perspectives.
- **Environment** – it can be seen that Sandra has scheduled a lunch meeting with a colleague at a location external to her workplace. This may be in part a response to lack of privacy and permissibility of such discussions within the workspace. Open-plan office spaces allow for regular interaction with colleagues but within a very public arena, whilst individual office spaces reduce natural interactions and in turn reduce the immediacy that is attractive with this kind of reflection.

The less formal aspects of reflection discussed above in many ways involve social workers seeking an alternative reflective relationship that either supplements or replaces that function in supervision. It is worth adding to this informal context the myriad of opportunities for self-reflection. This is covered in much greater detail elsewhere, but, given the relevant understanding of critical reflection, this can have all the benefits in terms of 'safety' and also encourage and develop intrinsic skills with which to increase self knowledge and aide the critically reflective practice. Yip (2006) notes the benefits of metaphorically unpeeling the onion of one's practice. By this Yip meant that given a culture of reflection, social workers can feel encouraged to unpick their beliefs, assumptions and feelings in relation to their practice, thus leading to reflexivity. What is interesting is the emphasis on self reflection being routed in a broader learning culture rather than easily existing on its own. This brings us back to the notion of a reflective organization (Morrison, 2007; Ruch, 2012) and the reflective tone that can be cascaded from an organizational level right down to individual reflection.

In many ways Sandra could fit self reflection into various parts of her working week. Moon (1999) notes the power of putting

Reflective Activity 9.4

1. Do you seek opportunities for reflection with peers? If so, what conditions facilitate this? If not, what are the barriers to such opportunities? What can you do about them?
2. Can you identify whether you work within a learning organisation? What are the messages and/or arrangements which communicate this to you? You might want to read Kerman et al (2012) before reflecting on this.
3. Do you write reflectively for your self or another audience? In terms of your ability to engage in critical reflection individually, what are the key challenges?

one's reflections down in written form. This will happen in part when Sandra writes her case notes for the two cases. The ordering, editing, prioritizing and analysing that goes into such a process has much in common with the key aspects of critical reflection. Sandra may equally undertake a degree of critical reflection in less structured non-work time such as whilst driving or, less ideally, whilst lying in bed at night. Yip (2006) provides a useful cautionary point in that self-reflection (when unsupported by other process of reflection) may run the risk of the development of a negative 'internal supervisor'. By this Yip means that if a social worker is struggling to manage aspects of their practice and is left to make judgments internally about their efficacy, then this can lead to an entrenched negative view of oneself, which can make reflection damaging rather than helpful.

Organizational culture and reflection

The discussion in this chapter has placed great emphasis on the role of individual motivations, opportunities and contexts. It is important to locate these discussions within the context of organizations. Organizations vary significantly in the way they operate and relate to the individuals within them. However, there are some elements that can be seen as central to any definition:

- **Social entities** – organizations are characterized and rely upon a degree of interaction and communication between individual people regardless of their level within the organization.

- **Goal-directed** – organizations evolve in response to a defined purpose or goal. For social work this is commonly related to the needs of a specific service user group
- **Structured** – flowing from the aforementioned 'goals', organizations develop processes and structures to facilitate the achievement of the goals.
- **Externally influenced** – organizations do not exist within a vacuum and are inevitably influenced and shaped by external factors. In relation to social work this may include professional codes, legislation, resources and user-group context.

For the purposes of this discussion, it may be useful to locate this chapter within the two opposing paradigms of scientific management approaches and human relations approaches. A scientific approach to a social work organization would involve rigid procedures which lock individual workers into highly specific roles and remits, and minimize (or indeed remove) the autonomy or strategic influence of individuals (Hafford-Letchfield, 2009). Such an organizational structure is goal-orientated, and reflects a managerialist and authoritarian conception of organizations.

Cole (1995) suggests that a human relations approach places much greater emphasis on the contribution and morale of the individuals involved in an organization, and values the relationship between said individuals and the wider goals of the organization. It is useful at this stage to draw on the seminal work of McGregor (1960) and the notion of 'Theory X and Theory Y' constructs of human relations within organizations. Simply put, 'Theory X' approaches fit the aforementioned scientific paradigm, placing an emphasis on employee control and manifesting lack of confidence in individual abilities and autonomy. 'Theory Y' approaches would reflect a more organic approach to human relations whereby there is an emphasis on professional development, empowerment and individual influence throughout the organization. The latter example has much to offer and underpins a social work organization which supports opportunities for critical reflection. It is easy to see how these two approaches can be played out in the focus and remit of social work supervision.

The paradigms introduced above would appear to reflect the familiar debates about the tensions between managerialist approaches and those which promote and encourage autonomy and professional discretion (Ferguson, 2005; Munro, 2011). Acknowledgement and reflection about the nature of the organizations and teams that social workers operate within is crucial to understanding and addressing the opportunities for meaningful and critical reflection. In relation to Sandra, it is clear that she would benefit from an organizational culture which facilitated both formal and informal opportunities for critical reflection and encouraged her to feel able to identify and examine her issues relating to her practice. Where such permissions are absent or opaque, we can see how easily Sandra would be left to repress, ignore or try to cope with the uncertainties and complexities of practice on her own.

Conclusion

The centrality of relationships with service users is underlined by the structure of this chapter. It is clear that the need for opportunities to critically reflect is demonstrated by experiences of direct practice. Our model (see Chapter 1) takes as a given the 'hard' contextual features such as legislation, theory and policy relating to the two cases presented in the case study. What the model allows for are the bespoke reactions and issues arising from the relationships within them. The responses of Sandra were purposely chosen to be contrasting in this chapter (positive identification versus anger), yet the role of critical reflection in terms of examining, managing and using the values and emotional dimensions are equally cogent in the two cases.

In this chapter we have explored the potential challenges for uniting the individual and organizational aspects of supervision. Linking back to the model, and considering the content of all the preceding practice-based chapters, shows that any supervision arrangement which neglects the 'soft' features of practice such as relationship dynamics and emotions simply overlooks a core aspect of the reality of social work practice, and as such is not fully fit for purpose.

This chapter has sought to locate critical reflection within a range of forums. It is evident that there is potentially a range of options open to Sandra, but that these are dependent on the culture and context of the organization in which she works. The breadth of the examples given emphasizes that the opportunity for critical reflection can be found in many places, but that organizational factors have a key influence regardless of the motivations and abilities of the individual worker. It is crucial that social workers are able to critically analyse the individual and structural factors which may affect their opportunities for reflection, as ultimately this will feed back into the quality of the practice and the relationships with the people who use social work services.

Further resources

Kerman, B., Freundlich, M., Law, J. and Brenner, E. (2012) 'Learning while doing in the human services: becoming a learning organization through organizational change', *Administration in Social Work*, 36(3), 234–257.
Describes the case of an organization which was able to establish a stronger infrastructure as a learning organization, leading to a better service provision for children.

Beddoe, L. (2010) 'Surveillance or reflection: Professional supervision in the risk society', *British Journal of Social Work*, 40, 1279–1296.
Beddoe undertakes a study looking at the nature of social work supervision in the context of risk. A key message concerns the desirability for workers to engage in reflection and 'be held' through the uncertainties of practice.

O'Donoghue, K. & Tsui, M. (2012) 'In search of an informed supervisory practice: An exploratory study', *Practice: Social Work in Action*, 24:1, ??20
Examines the perspectives of supervisors and explores the sources of knowledge which inform their approaches to supervision.

CHAPTER 10

From a reflective social work practitioner to a reflective social work organization

In this book, especially Chapters 3 to 9, the authors consciously deconstructed the processes of social work practice, to engage the reader in an in-depth understanding of the role of reflection and reflexivity. Different aspects of social work practice were also related to the 'hard' features and the soft features discussed in Chapters 1 and 2. Similarly, the case studies highlighted particular dimensions of a social worker's practice. In reality, the same social worker would undertake all aspects of practice, namely assessment, intervention, attending meetings, communicating, making decisions related to risk and interacting in support and supervision.

Any one of the case studies presented in Chapters 2 to 9 could have been extended to include all the dimensions. For example, consider the case study in Chapters 4 and 5. Steve, the social worker, would have engaged in effective communication (Chapter 3) with Dot to find out her wishes with regards to management of care to be able to assess her needs and wishes (Chapter 4) and to put an intervention in place (Chapter 5). This would have led to a cycle of reflection, and perhaps reading up on legislation, theories of empowerment and literature on relationship between choice and wellbeing, followed by a discussion with peers or his supervisor (Chapter 9). This then would have resulted in writing of case notes for Dot using appropriate strategies for effective recording of the decision (Chapter 8; and perhaps after careful consideration of the risks involved, Chapter 6). He would then be involved in a meeting with Dot, her family, another social worker if he was to pass the case on to, for example, Tracy (Chapter 5), or health care professionals (Chapter 7). He would need to use reflexivity to understand the power dynamics in these meetings and to be able to assert Dot's view point to others (Chapter 7). He might experience various emotional responses to the changing situations as well needs to be able to understand and manage others' emotional response. Similarly, he might need to consciously examine his own values and their impact on his decisions or interactions with others. Further, over time, he might find that the situation has changed for Dot or that she has changed her mind and wants to move into residential care. This would lead to going back to assessment and the start of all the processes again.

Features of reflective social work practice

As mentioned in Chapters 1 and 2, there are some 'hard' features of social work practice, namely policy, procedures, legislation and theories. These provide the framework within which the social worker can develop the 'soft' features such as reflection, emotion and values. Although in Chapter 1 these have been separated, in the real world it is impossible to do so. For example, critical reflection that a social worker might engage in will require them to take cognizance of the 'hard' features. These 'hard' features might again act as restricting or supportive factors leading to consideration of personal and professional values, and any resulting emotional responses.

Further, as was seen during the consideration of reflexivity, it is important to understand not only the influence of 'hard' features on the social work practice, but also to consider the impact of the social worker (individually or as a group) on the 'hard' features such as policy. Also, as highlighted in several chapters, it has been suggested that a critically reflective social work practitioner will challenge the power dynamics, group think and underlying assumptions (White et al., 2006). Several chapters have asked the reader to consider the current policy, theory and research to legitimize their focus on 'soft' features. For example, earlier in this chapter it was suggested that Steve might find it useful to make a case for Dot's wishes to be acknowledged by reading up on legislation, theories of empowerment and literature on relationship between choice and wellbeing. Similarly, in Chapter 6, the authors have talked about Erika reading about need being as important as risk, and making links between the desistance literature and what she wanted to do.

Therefore, what this book is highlighting is that an effective social work practitioner is one who examines every angle of a situation and uses various sources to inform their practice. The evidence will come from several directions, such as the service users, reflection on the interaction with the service user, policy, professional codes etc. As a well-balanced practitioner they will need to explore every source of information, analysing and reflecting on each individually and in the ways they conspire together. Instead of then relying on the 'hard' and tangible features and moving towards being rational-technical, they will undertake double-loop learning, which leads to learning not only for that context but also future contexts; this learning will be based on the clear understanding and articulation of values and emotions through critical reflection and reflexivity. Also, this learning will be on-going, with multiple cycles of action and reflection embedded in it.

Further, recently policy, at least in the UK context, is moving from being procedurally focussed to relying more on social workers' discretion. There is a focus on increased autonomy and an acknowledgement of relationship building being core to social work practice. Similarly, BASW's Code of Ethics (BASW, 2012) and the Professional Capabilities Framework (College of Social Work, 2012) explicitly mention reflection. Similarly, research evidence and theories are increasingly emphasizing the development of a critically reflective social worker and a reflective organization (Raelin, 2001; Ferguson, 2005; Nolte, 2010). In other words, there is a well-intentioned theoretical and policy direction of travel towards embracing the 'soft' features of practice. Chapters 3 to 9 have attempted to translate that theory and policy into action.

Professionalism

Another theme that has been touched on in many chapters is that of professionalism. Chapter 2 highlights the concerns of the social worker Belaku who was embarrassed when he got upset in a meeting. This came from his notion of others seeing him as not being 'professional'. The registration requirement of the professional body is that all practitioners or students on professional training programmes should be 'professional'. However, what does becoming a professional imply? Is it the completion of a programme of study and a degree that one receives at the end of it? The College of Social Work's (2012) Professional Capabilities Framework, has nine domains including professionalism, values and ethics, and critical reflection and analysis. The first domain, professionalism, highlights that social workers' title is a legislative title and as 'members of an internationally recognised profession... social workers demonstrate professional commitment by taking responsibility for their conduct, practice and learning, with support through supervision ... Take responsibility for obtaining regular, effective supervision from a SW for effective practice, reflection and career development... Maintain professionalism in the face of more challenging circumstances'.

However, a thorough examination of the website fails to discover a clearly set-out definition of professional or professionalism. This then leaves the conceptualization of 'being a professional' or 'professionalism' open to interpretation. So, is a professional a person who is aligned to a professional body, has a distinct and recognized profession, and who follows the key capabilities of that profession at levels appropriate to their stage and experience in that profession? This is not the case for social work alone. Previous research in other professions indicates that there is a lack of a clear definition of professionalism and Evetts (2012) suggests that the conceptualization of professionalism in recent years has changed from occupational professionalism to organizational professionalism; that is instead of upholding professional values, there is a move towards top-down control. Within this uncertainty and organizational professionalism, practitioners have been seen to interpret professionalism as the ability to be detached, to be able to do one's work without being influenced by instincts and overall ignore or overcome any complexities and uncertainties that might be apparent in the work (Parton, 2003). Therefore, the 'professional' becomes a person who can act in a scientific manner and be able to predict the outcomes.

However, as discussed in Chapter 6, Littlechild (2010) in the context of child protection highlights the falseness of the assumption that a social worker can do that. In our view, the social work professional has to be able to deal with inevitable uncertainties associated with human interaction, be flexible in their dealings with each individual, and more importantly understand their own impact on the practice and profession. Therefore, the authors of this book consider professionalism to be the *ability to* be reflective and reflexive, be cognitively flexible, and be emotionally intelligent. In order to achieve this, they must be able to understand and respond according to the underpinning values and principles, and make informed decisions in the context of all the 'soft' and 'hard' features of social work; therefore engaging in lifelong learning both through cycles of reflection individually and as an organization. However, most importantly, this professional should be able to use critical reflection to challenge dominant conceptualizations of professionalism (or the ones suggested by the authors for that matter!) to consider the most appropriate concepts in the context of their work. Ideally, this critical reflection should happen at an organizational level so that there is a move from hierarchical organizational professionalism to occupational professionalism informed by everybody in the organization. Also, it is important to recognize that to be a *professional* social worker, the relationship with the service user is central and should be the defining feature of this profession (Fenton and Walker, 2012).

Relationship-based work

One of the key themes to emerge from the preceding chapters is the importance of relationship-based work. Social workers work in close contact with service users, and research suggests that close relationships and good understanding can lead to positive outcomes (see Chapter 7). Clemans (2004) highlights the satisfaction that social workers feel by supporting a service user through a difficult life experience or by working collaboratively with other professionals. In other words, they experience 'Compassion Satisfaction' (Stamm, 2002). However, there is another, more complex, aspect to this relationship-based work, especially in the context of the service users experiencing trauma. Bride's (2007) study with nearly 300 social workers randomly selected from around 3000 social workers in one area of the US found that 97 per cent of social workers said that their service users had experienced trauma and 88.9 per cent indicated that they were involved in issues associated with that trauma. This suggests that a large number of social workers may be exposed to the trauma of service users as a result of their role. The Secondary Traumatic Stress Scale showed that 70 per cent of the participant social workers reported experiencing at least one secondary traumatic symptom in the last week, with 15 per cent meeting the criteria for a diagnosis of post-traumatic stress disorder, which is nearly twice that of the general population (Bride, 2007). This can then lead to 'compassion fatigue' (Stamm, 2002), which can result in the social worker becoming detached and less empathetic towards the service users.

Further, the pressures from outside the organization can be immense. As highlighted in Chapter 6, if there is an undesirable outcome, the government becomes controlling and organizations become risk-averse. The organizational culture might heighten the notion of 'safety first', which might reduce the autonomy and discretion of the social worker. For social workers who are working in such complex situations, not only are the relations with the service users important; those with other professionals become important too. As was seen in Chapters 3 and 7, communication in different contexts, especially interprofessional meetings, can be fraught with tensions. In that environment, in a context where social workers' practice is already seen to be 'namby-pamby', an individual social worker might find it difficult to stand up against their organization or others in interprofessional meetings. This might lead to discomfort as they might not be able to function in a way that is most aligned to their value base. This could add further stress to social workers, even when not dealing with service users who have experienced severe trauma.

Therefore, it is important that social workers are appropriately supported within their own organizations as '…without self-care and an attuned agency and profession, the benefits of the work may soon dissipate for workers and, in turn, clients' (Clemans, 2004, p. 3). The chapters in this book have also repeatedly emphasized the importance of a safe environment in which social workers can critically reflect on-practice and for-practice. Based on the SuReCom model, Figure 9.1 in Chapter 9 provides a model that can be used as a tool to ensure that this safe and supportive environment can be created through transparent and mutually agreed supervisory relationship. Further, Chapter 2 suggests that social workers might consider reflective dialogues with peers and critical friends, or use a double-entry journal, where they can reflect with support from a critical friend.

Reflective organizations

So far what has been raised in the chapters, as well as the reflective models, is the notion of an individual becoming a critically reflective social worker. For an organizational environment that supports critical reflection and reflexivity, it is important that not only individuals engage in these softer features: everybody in the organization needs to be proactive in creating a reflective organization (Nolte, 2010). Ferguson (2005) also emphasizes the importance of creating organizational cultures that are reflective in nature. For this to happen there has to be a move from individualized reflection to reflection in teams as part of a social process (Hoyrup, 2004). As mentioned in Chapter 2, practitioners interviewed in Jindal-Snape and Holmes (2009) indicated that they preferred reflecting in a dialogue with peers. This social nature of reflection is further emphasized in Chapter 9 with its focus on reflection in support and supervision.

However, reflection with others as critical friends and supervisor is slightly different from the concept of *collective reflection*, with its emphasis on everybody *reflecting together*. This collective process has been emphasized by organizational theorists. Strategies for developing a reflective organization have been suggested that involve reflective actions, building communities, process improvement, learning teams and culture of learning (Raelin, 2001, 2002). When applied to a social work context, these would equate to colleagues generating others' interest in reflective practice as well as teaching each other reflective skills; sharing and testing ideas through communities of practice or in support and supervision; reinforcing experiential learning that is discussed with others; developing learning teams where individuals can discuss dilemma and consider them in the context of relevant theory, research evidence or policy; and reflective practice becoming a way of life that is modelled by senior management.

Raelin (2002) and Hoyrup (2004) synthesized Van Woerkom's (2003) key preconditions for Critical Reflective Work Behaviour (CRWB) to happen in an organizational context; namely sharing knowledge and vision, learning from mistakes, challenging 'group think' (also see Chapter 7), and asking for feedback. Further, these have to happen publicly within an organization. As can be seen, these are aspects that should remove the 'defensive strategies' (Chapter 7) and social workers will not be able to operate in a climate of preponderance of win/lose thinking. Rather, openness, admitting to ones mistakes and seeing them as opportunities to reflect on and learn from will become the norm. Again, as discussed in Chapter 2, this requires a cognitively flexible social worker as well as an organization where everybody values critical reflection and cognitive flexibility.

Although the organizational culture needs to be supportive and flexible, social workers have to remember that the organizations are not separate entities; *they* are the organization and *they* contribute to the organizational culture. Seeing organizational culture as a given might indicate that one is caught up in single-loop learning, as discussed in Chapter 2. A critically reflection social worker would see themselves as major actors in changing the organizational culture.

Conclusion

It is time to revisit the Reflective Social Work Practitioner Model. The preceding chapters and this model focus on an individual reflective social work practitioner. It is unrealistic to expect that every practitioner takes responsibility for becoming critically reflective without cognizance of other practitioners in their organization. It is important to realize that the sum total of all professionals reflecting will not make a reflective organization. Certain preconditions, as suggested earlier, have to be in place. In conclusion, the authors' would like to consider how this model would manifest within a reflective organization. Using the reflective social work practitioner model (Figure 1.1) as its basis, Figure 10.1 illustrates what a reflective organization might look like.

The two circles in Figure 10.1 represent individual critically reflective social workers. However, for these individual social workers to collectively reflect and create a reflective organization, certain preconditions are required, as illustrated by the words in bold around the two reflective social workers. The lines and text between the two reflective social workers show the processes through which this could be achieved. As can be seen from Figure 10.1, a reflective organization requires critically reflective social workers within an organizational culture that values sharing knowledge and vision, learning from mistakes, challenging the established assumptions and group think, and cognitive and organizational flexibility. These can be achieved by creating space and time for team reflection, effective supervision (perhaps following Figure 9.1) and creation of an emotionally supportive environment.

Readers might reflect on how reflective their organization is and consider ways of making it more reflective. This could be done through a simple tool, as indicated in Table 10.1.

This grid is a template which can be developed based on the requirements or context of a particular organization. On the left-hand side we list all the possible contexts, and across are the key features or attributes of a reflective organization. The idea is to try to identify where the organization might be, on a scale of 1 to 5, '1' showing that the key features are not very evident and '5' showing that they are very evident, with the purpose of moving towards 5. In an organization, colleagues could reflect and complete the template individually, and then bring their ratings to the big group for discussion; or do it as a collective exercise from the start. It

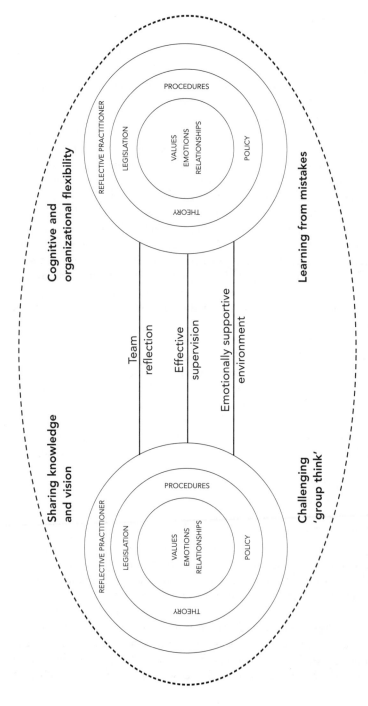

Figure 10.1 The Reflective Social Work Organization Model

Table 10.1 Grid to evaluate 'How reflective is my organization?'

Settings	Open discussion	Sharing knowledge	Sharing vision	Acknowledgement of mistakes and lessons learned	Challenging and debating	Flexibility in thinking and systems	Opportunity to discuss feelings	Opportunity to discuss personal values	Responsive	Acceptance of risk and uncertainty
Communication with • service users • peers • other professionals										
Meetings • service users • peers • other professionals										
Assessment										
Intervention										
Decision making										
Support and Supervision										
Records and case notes										

Rating: 1 to 5, with 1 being not evident at all and 5 being very evident might be a good exercise to return to several times a year with clear learning and action points emerging from each cycle of collective reflection.

Finally, the authors hope that the book and different chapters have provided the readers with an insight into the importance of becoming a critically reflective social work practitioner, who is able to be reflexive about their values and emotions, and their impact on practice. Also, the hope is that they will move beyond that to create a critically reflective organization which will be able to work well with the 'hard' and 'soft' features of their practice to make a real difference to the lives of the service users.

References

Argyris, C. and Schön, D. (1974) *Theory in practice: Increasing professional effectiveness* (San Francisco: Jossey-Bass).

Atkins, S. and Murphy, K. (1994) 'Reflective practice', *Nursing Standard*, 8(39), 49–56.

Banks, S. (2006) *Ethics and values in social work* (Basingstoke: Palgrave Macmillan).

Banks, S. (2012) *Ethics and Values in social work*, 4th Edition (Basingstoke: Palgrave Macmillan).

Barrett, L. (2012) 'Emotions are real', *Emotion*, 12(3), 413–429.

Barry, M. (2007) *Effective approaches to risk assessment in social work: An international literature review* (Edinburgh: Scottish Executive).

Bassot, B. (2013) *The reflective journal* (Basingstoke: Palgrave Macmillan).

Beckett, C. (2010) *Assessment and Intervention in social work: Preparing for practice* (London: Sage).

Beddoe, L. (2010) 'Surveillance or reflection: Professional supervision in the risk society', *British Journal of Social Work*, 40, 1279–1296.

Bissell, G. (2012) *Organisational behaviour for social work* (Bristol: Policy Press).

Bogo, M. and McKnight, K. (2006) 'Clinical supervision in social work – a review of the research literature', *The Clinical Supervisor*, 24, 49–67.

Bolton, G. (2010) *Reflective practice: Writing and professional development* (London: SAGE).

Bolton, S. and Boyd, C. (2003) 'Trolley dolly or skilled emotion manager? Moving on from Hochschild's Managed Heart', *Work, Employment and Society*, 17(2), 289–308.

Borton, T. (1970) *Reach, teach and touch* (London: McGraw Hill).

Bride, B. (2007) 'Prevalence of secondary traumatic stress amongst social workers', *Social Work*, 52(1), 63–70.

British Association of Social Workers (BASW) (2012) *The code of ethics for social work: Statement of principles* (Birmingham: BASW).

Broadhurst, K., Wastell, D., White, S., Hall, C., Peckover, S., Thompson, K., Pithouse, A. and Davey, D. (2010) 'Performing 'Initial Assessment': Identifying the latent conditions for error at the front-door of Local Authority Children's Services', *British Journal of Social Work*, 40, 352–370 .

Brodie, I., Nottingham, C. and Plunkett, S. (2008) 'A tale of two reports: Social work in Scotland from *Social Work and the Community* to *Changing Lives* (2006)', *British Journal of Social Work*, 38, 697–715.

Calder, M. C. (2003) 'Child Protection Conferences: A framework for chairperson preparation,' *Child Care in Practice*, 9(1), 32–48.

Calderwood, K., Harper, K., Ball, K. and Laing, D. (2009) 'When values and behaviour conflict: Immigrant BSW students' experiences revealed', *Journal of Ethical and Cultural Diversity in Social Work*, 18, 110–128.

Carson, D. (1996) 'Risking legal repercussions', in H. Kemshall and J. Pritchard (eds.) *Good practice in risk assessment and management* (London: Jessica Kingsley), 3–12.

CGC/CCW. (2004) Code of practice: Standards for social care workers and their managers. http://www.ccwales.org.uk/code-of-practice-for-workers/
Download *Code of practice – Pictorial version* (pdf) (Accessed 13 October 2013).

Christ, G.H. and Sormanti, M. (2000) 'Advancing social work practice in end of life care', *Social Work in Heath Care*, 30(2), 81–99.

Cleaver, H., Walker, S., Scott, J., Cleaver, D., Rose, W., Ward, H. and Pithouse, A. (2008) *The integrated children's system enhancing social work and inter agency practice* (London: Jessica Kingsley Publishers).

Clemans, S. (2004) 'Understanding vicarious traumatisation – strategies for social workers', *Social Work Today*, 4(2), 13–17.

Cm 5730 (2003) *The Victoria Climbié Inquiry Report* (London: The Stationery Office).

Cole, G. (1995) *Organisational behaviour: Theory and practice* (London: DP Publications).

College of Social Work. (2012) *The Professional Capabilities Framework*. http://www.tcsw.org.uk/professional-capabilities-framework/?terms=capabilities%20framework (Accessed 13 October 2013).

Corby, B. (2006) *Child abuse: Toward a knowledge base*, 3rd Edition (Maidenhead: Open University Press).

Criminal Justice Act (2003), http://www.legislation.gov.uk/all?title=criminal%20justice%20act%202003 (Accessed 13 October 2013).

Crisp, B.R., Anderson, M.R., Orme, J. and Green Lister, P. (2007) 'Assessment frameworks: A critical reflection', *British Journal of Social Work*, 37, 1059–1077.

Crisp, B., Lister, P. and Dutton, K. (2005) *Evaluation of an innovative method of assessment: Critical Incident Analysis* (Glasgow: Scottish Institute for Excellence in Social Work).

Damasio, A. (1994) *Descartes' error: Emotion, reason and the human brain* (New York: Putnam).

Data Protection Act (1998) http://www.legislation.gov.uk/ukpga/1998/29/contents (accessed 11 October 2013).

Department of Children, Schools and Families (2009) *Building a safe, confident future: The final report of the social work task force* (London: Department of Children, Schools and Families).

Department of Health (DoH) (2000) *The framework for the Assessment of children in need and their families* (London: The Stationery Office).

Department of Health (DoH) (2012), *Caring for our future: Reforming care and support* (London: DoH).

Devitt, B., Philip, J. and McLachlan, S. (2010) 'Team dynamics, decision making, and attitudes toward multidisciplinary cancer meetings: Health professionals' perspectives', *Journal of Oncology Practice*, 6(6), 17–20.

Di Franks, N.N. (2008) 'Social workers and the NASW Code of Ethics: Belief, behaviour and disjuncture', *Social Work*, 53, 167–176.

Doel, M. (2006) *Using groupwork* (Abingdon: Routledge).

Dole, M. and Marsh, P. (1992) *Task-centred social work* (Aldershot: Ashgate).

Dominelli. L. (2009) 'Anti-oppressive practice: Challenges of the 21st century', in R. Adams, L. Dominelli and M. Payne (eds.) *Social work. Themes, issues and critical debates* (3rd edition) (Basingstoke: Palgrave Macmillan), 49–64.

Evetts, J. (2012) 'Professionalism in turbulent times: Changes, challenges and opportunities', Propel International Conference, 9–11 May 2012, Stirling, UK.

Farrall, S. (2002) *Rethinking what works with offenders: Probation, social context and desistance from crime* (Portland: Willan Publishing).

Featherstone, B. (2010) 'Ethic of care', in M. Gray and S. Webb (eds.), *Ethics and value perspectives in social work* (Basingstoke: Palgrave Macmillan), 73–84.

Fenton, J. (2012) 'Bringing together messages from the literature on criminal justice social work and 'disjuncture': The importance of helping', *British Journal of Social Work*, 42, 941–956.

Fenton, J. (2013) 'Risk aversion and anxiety in Scottish criminal justice social work: Can desistance and human rights agendas have an impact?', *Howard Journal of Criminal Justice*, 52, 77–90.

Fenton, J. and Walker, L. (2012) 'When is a personal care task not just a task? Can undertaking personal care within practice learning opportunities enhance the learning of student social workers?', *Journal of Practice Teaching and Learning*, 11(1), 19–36.

Ferguson, H. (2004) *Protecting children in time: Child abuse, child protection and the consequences of modernity* (Basingstoke: Palgrave Macmillan).

Ferguson, H. (2005) 'Working with violence, the emotions and the psychosocial dynamics of child protection: reflections on the Victoria Climbie case', *Social Work Education*, 24, 781–795.

Ferguson, H. (2010) 'Walks, home visits and atmospheres: risks and the everyday practices and mobilities of social work and child protection', *British Journal of Social Work*, 40, 1100–1117.

Fook, J. (2012) *Social work: A critical approach to practice* (Sage: London).

Fook, J. and Askeland, G., A. (2006) 'The 'critical' in critical reflection, in S. White, J. Fook and F. Gardner (eds.) *Critical reflection in health and social care* (Maidenhead: Open University Press), 40–54.

Fook, J. and Gardner, F. (2007) *Practising Critical Reflection. A Resource Handbook* (Maidenhead: Open University Press).

Gambrill, E. (2012) *Critical thinking in clinical practice*, 3rd edition (Chichester: Wiley).

Ghaffar, W., Manby, M. and Race, T. (2012) 'Exploring the experiences of parents and carers whose children have been subject to child protection plans', *British Journal of Social Work*, 42, 887–905.

Gibbs, G. (1988) *Learning by doing: A guide to teaching and learning methods* (Oxford: Further Education Unit, Oxford Brookes University).

Gibelman, M. and Schervish, P.H. (1997) *Who we are: A second look* (Washington, DC: NASW Press).

Goddard, C.R., Saunders, B.J. and Stanley, J.R. (1999) 'Structured Risk assessment procedures: Instruments of abuse?', *Child Abuse Review*, 8, 251–263.

Goleman, D. (1995) *Emotional intelligence: Why it can matter more than IQ* (New York: Bantam).

Gorman, H. (2000) 'Winning hearts and minds? Emotional labour and learning for care management work', *Journal of Social Work Practice*, 14, 149–158.

Gray, J. (2002) 'National policy on the assessment of children in need and their families', in H. Ward and W. Rose. (eds.), *Approaches to needs assessment in children's services* (London: Jessica Kingsley Publishers), 169–194.

Gregory, M. (2010) 'Reflection and resistance: probation practice and the ethic of care', *British Journal of Social Work*, 40, 2274–2290.

GSCC (2004) *Codes of practice for social care workers and employers.* http://www.skillsforcare.org.uk/developing_skills/GSCCcodesofpractice/GSCC_codes_of_practice.aspx Download *Codes of practice for social care workers* and *Codes of practice for employers of social care workers* (Accessed 13 October 2013).

Hafford-Letchfield, T. (2009) *Management and organisations in social work* (Exeter: Learning Matters).

Halliday, S., Burns, N., Hutton, N., McNeill, F. and Tata, C. (2009) 'Street level bureaucracy, interprofessional relations, and coping mechanisms: a study of criminal justice social workers in the sentencing process', *Law and Policy*, 31, 405–428.

Harding, T. and Beresford, P. (1995) *The standards we expect: what service users and carers want from social workers* (London: National Institute of Social Work).

Health and Care Professions Council (2012) Media and events. http://www.hpc-uk.org/mediaandevents/pressreleases/hpctobecome hcpcon1august2012/ (Accessed 13 October 2013).

Healy, K. and Mulholland, J. (2012) *Writing skills for social workers* (London: Sage).

Hennessey, R. (2011) *Relationship skills in social work* (London: Sage).

Heron, B. (2005) 'Self-reflection in critical social work practice: subjectivity and the possibilities of resistance', *Reflective Practice: International and Multidisciplinary Perspectives*, 6(3), 341–351.

Heron, G. and Murray, R. (2004) 'The place of writing in social work', *Journal of Social Work*, 4 (2), 199–214.

Hochschild, A. R. (1983) *The managed heart: Commercialization of human feeling* (Los Angeles: University of California Press).

Hodson, A.V. (2011) 'Pre-birth assessment in social work', unpublished PhD Thesis (Huddersfield: University of Huddersfield).

Hodson, A.V. and Deery, R. (2014) 'Protecting unborn babies: ethical considerations for social work and midwifery', in D. Jindal-Snape and E.F. Hannah (eds.), *Dynamics of personal, professional and interprofessional ethics* (Bristol: Policy Press).

Hopkins, G. (1998) *Plain English for social services* (Dorset: Russell House).

Horner, N. (2009) 'Understanding Intervention', in R. Adams, L. Dominelli and M. Payne (eds.), *Social work themes, issues and critical debates* (Basingstoke: Palgrave Macmillan), 244–260.

Horwath, J. (2007) *Child neglect: identification and assessment* (Basingstoke: Palgrave Macmillan).

Horwath, J. (2011) 'See the practitioner, see the child: *The Framework for the Assessment of Children in Need and Their Families* ten years on', *British Journal of Social Work*, 41(6), 1070–1087.

Howe, D. (2008) *The emotionally intelligent social worker* (Basingstoke, Palgrave Macmillan).

Hoyrup, C. (2004) 'Reflection as a core process in organisational learning', *The Journal of Workplace Learning*, 16(8), 442–454.

Hudson, B. (2001) 'Human rights, public safety and the probation service: defending justice in the risk society', *The Howard Journal*, 40, 103–113.

Ingram, R. (2012a) 'Emotions, social work practice and supervision: An uneasy alliance?', *Journal of Social Work Practice*, 27(1), 5–19.

Ingram, R. (2012b) 'Emotions and social work practice', unpublished PhD thesis (Dundee: University of Dundee).

Ingram, R. (2013) 'Locating emotional intelligence at the heart of social work practice,' *British Journal of Social Work*, 43, 987–1004.

International Federation of Social Work (IFSW) (2013) *Definition of social work* [online] http://ifsw.org/policies/definition-of-social-work/ (Accessed 13 October 2013).

Jackson, L. (2000) *Child sexual abuse in Victorian England* (London: Routledge)

James, W. (1890) 'The principles of psychology', in J. Jenkins, K. Oatley and N. Stein(eds.), *Human emotions: A reader* (Oxford: Blackwell), 21–30.

Jindal-Snape, D. and Hannah E.F. (2014) 'Understanding the dynamics of personal, professional and interprofessional ethics: A possible way forward', in D. Jindal-Snape and E.F. Hannah (eds.), *Dynamics of personal, professional and interprofessional ethics* (Bristol: Policy Press).

Jindal-Snape, D. and Holmes, E.A. (2009) 'Experience of reflection during transition from higher education to professional practice', *Reflective Practice: International and multidisciplinary perspectives*, 10(2), 219–232.

Jindal-Snape, D. and Ingram, R. (2013) 'Understanding and Supporting Triple Transitions of International Doctoral Students: ELT and SuReCom Models', *Journal of Perspectives in Applied Academic Practice*, 1(1), 17–24.

Johns, C. (1994) 'Nuances of Reflection', *Journal of Clinical Nursing*, 3, 71–75.

Jones, C. (2001) 'Voices from the front line: state social workers and new labour.' *British Journal of Social Work*, 31, 547–562.

Kadushin, A. (1976) *Supervision in social work* (New York: Columbia University Press).

Kadushin, A. and Harkness, D. (2002) *Supervision in social work*, 3rd edition (New York: Columbia University Press).

Keen, S., Gray, I., Parker, J., Galpin, D. and Brown, K. (2009) *Newly qualified social workers: A handbook for practice* (Exeter: Learning Matters).

Kemshall, H. (2002) *Risk, social policy and welfare* (Buckingham: Open University Press).

Kerman, B., Freundlich, M., Law, J. and Brenner, E. (2012) 'Learning while doing in the human services: becoming a learning organization through organizational change', *Administration in Social Work*, 36 (3), 234–257.

Kolb, D. (1984) *Experiential learning: Experience as a source of learning and development* (New Jersey: Prentice Hall).

Koprowska, J. (2005) *Communication and interpersonal skills in social work* (Exeter: Learning Matters).

Kosny, A. and Eakin, J. (2008) 'The hazards of helping: work, mission and risk in non-profit social services organizations', *Health, Risk and Society*, 10, 149–166.

Lay, S. and McGuire, L. (2010) 'Building a lens for critical reflection and reflexivity in social work education', *Social Work Education*, 29(5), 539–550.

Lazarus, R. (1991) 'Emotion and adaptation', in J. Jenkins, K. Oatley, and N. Stein (eds.), *Human emotions: a reader* (Oxford: Blackwell), 38–45.

LeDoux, J. (1997) *The emotional brain: The mysterious underpinnings of emotional life* (New York: Simon & Schuster).

Lishman, J. (2009) *Communication in social work* (Basingstoke: Palgrave Macmillan).

Littlechild, B. (2010) 'Child protection social work: risks of fears and fears of risk – impossible tasks from impossible goals?', *Social Policy and Administration*, 42, 662–675.

Liu, F. and Maitlis, S. (2013) 'Emotional dynamics and strategizing processes: A study of strategic conversations in top team meetings', *Journal of Management Studies*, DOI: 10.1111/j.1467–6486.2012. 01087.x.

MacDonald, G. (1990) 'Allocating blame in social work', *British Journal of Social Work*, 20, 525–546.

MacDonald, G. and MacDonald, K. (2010) 'Safeguarding: a case for intelligent risk management', *British Journal of Social Work*, 40, 1174–1191.

Management of Offenders etc (Scotland) Act 2005, http://www. legislation.gov.uk/asp/2005/14/contents (Accessed 13 October 2013).

Mattison, M. (2000) 'Ethical decision making: the person in the process', *Social Work*, 45, 201–211.

McCulloch, T. and McNeill, F. (2008) 'Desistance-focused approaches', in S. Green, E. Lancaster and S. Feasey (eds.), *Addressing offending behaviour: context, practice and values* (Devon: Willan), 154–171.

McGregor, D. (1960) *The human side of enterprise* (London: McGraw-Hill).

McNeill, F., Batchelor, S., Burnett, R. and Knox, J. (2005) *21st-century social work, reducing re-offending: Key practice skills* (Edinburgh: Scottish Government).

Meagher, G and Parton, N. (2004) 'Modernising social work and the ethics of care', *Social Work and Society*, 2 (1)10–27.

Milner, J. and O'Byrne, P. (2009) *Assessment in social work*, 3rd edition (Basingstoke: Palgrave Macmillan).

Ministry of Justice (2012) http://www.justice.gov.uk/downloads/ offenders/mappa/mappa-guidance-2012-part1.pdf (Accessed 13 October 2013).

Moon, J. (1999) *Reflection in learning and professional development* (Abingdon: RoutledgeFalmer).

Moon, J. (2004) *A handbook of reflective and experiential learning: Theory and practice* (Abingdon: RoutledgeFalmer).

Morrison, T. (2007) 'Emotional intelligence, emotion and social work: Context, characteristics, complications and contribution', *The British Journal of Social Work*, 37, 245–263.

Mullender, A. and Perrott, S. (2002) 'Social work and organisations', in R. Adams, L. Dominelli and M. Payne (eds.) *Social work: themes issues and critical debates* (Basingstoke: Palgrave Macmillan), 74–83.

Munro, E. (2011) *The Munro review of child protection: Final report* (London: TSO).

NISSC (2004) Codes of practice for social care workers and employers of social care workers. http://www.niscc.info/codes_of_practice-10.aspx (Accessed 13 October 2013).

Nolte, H. (2010) 'Reflective organization', *Cybernetics and Human Knowing*, 17(1–2), 77–91.

Noonan, W.R. (2007) *Discussing the undiscussable: A guide to overcoming defensive routines in the workplace* (San Francisco, CA: Jossey-Bass Business & Management).

Oatley, K. (2004) *Emotions: A brief history* (Oxford: Blackwell Publishing).

O'Brien, S. (2003) *Report of the Caleb Ness Inquiry* (Edinburgh: Edinburgh and Lothians Child Protection Committee).

O'Donnell, P., Farrar, A., Brintzenhofeszoc, K., Conrad, A. P., Danis, M., Grady, C., Taylor, C. and Ulrich, C. (2008) 'Predictors of ethical stress, moral action and job satisfaction in health care social workers', *Social Work in Health Care*, 46, 29–51.

O'Donoghue, K.. & Tsui, M,. (2012) 'In Search of an informed supervisory practice: An exploratory study', *Practice Social Work in Action*, 24:1, 3–20

Pagliari, C. and Grimshaw, J. (2002) 'Impact of group structure and process on multidisciplinary evidence-based guideline development: an observational study,' *Journal of Evaluation in Clinical Practice*, 8(2), 145–153.

Park, J.J. and Millora, M.L. (2012) 'The relevance of reflection: An empirical examination of the role of reflection in ethics of caring, leadership, and psychological well-being', *Journal of College Student Development*, 53(2), 221–242.

Parker, J. and Bradley, G. (2010) *Social work practice: Assessment, planning, intervention and review,* 3rd edition (Exeter: Learning Matters).

Parton, N. (2003) 'Rethinking professional practice: The contributions of social constructionism and the feminist "ethics of care"', *British Journal of Social Work*, 33, 1–6.

Parton, N. (2006) *Safeguarding childhood. Early intervention and surveillance in a late modern society* (Basingstoke: Palgrave Macmillan).

Parton, N. (2007) 'Safeguarding children: a socio-historical analysis' in K. Wilson and A. James (eds.), *The child protection handbook*, 3rd edition (Amsterdam: Elsevier), 9–30.

Payne, M. (2005) *Modern social work theory* (Basingstoke: Palgrave Macmillan).

Philips, D. (2009) 'Beyond the risk agenda', in S. Green, E. Lancaster and S. Feasey (eds.), *Addressing offending behaviour: Context, practice and values* (Devon: Willan), 172–189.

Preston-Shoot, M. (2003) 'Changing learning and learning change,' *Journal of Social Work Practice*, 17(1), 9–23.

Prince, K. (1996) *Boring records: Communication, speech and writing in social work*. London: Jessica Kingsley.

Raelin, J. (2001) 'Public reflection as the basis for learning', *Management Learning*, 32(1), 11–30.

Raelin, J. (2002) '"I don't have time to think!" (vs. The art of reflective practice)', *Reflections: The SoL Journal on Knowledge, Learning, and Change*, 4(1), 66–79.

Reamer, F. and Shardlow, S. (2009) 'Ethical codes of practice in the US and UK: One profession, two standards,' *The Journal of Social Work Values and Ethics*, Volume 6, 2. np http://www.socialworker.com/jswve/content/view/120/68/ [Accessed 13 October 2013).

Redmond, B. (2006) *Reflection in action: Developing reflective practice in health and social services* (Aldershot: Ashgate).

Reynolds, W. J. and Scott, B. (1999) 'Empathy: a crucial component of the helping relationship', *Journal of Psychiatric and Mental Health Nursing*, 6, 363–370.

Rosenberg, M. (1990) 'Reflexivity and emotions', *Social Psychology Quarterly*, 53(1), 3–12.

Ruch, G. (2009) 'Identifying "the critical" in a relationship-based model of reflection', *European Journal of Social Work*, 12, 349–362.

Ruch, G. (2012) 'Where have all the feelings gone? Developing reflective relationship-based management in child-care social work', *British Journal of Social Work*, 42(7), 1315–1332.

Salovey, P. and Mayer, J. (1990) 'Emotional intelligence', *Imagination, Cognition and Personality*, 9, 185–211.

Sawyer, A. (2009) 'Mental health workers negotiating risk on the front line', *Australian Social Work* , 62, 441–459.

Schon, D. (1983) *The reflective practitioner: How professionals think in action* (New York: Basic Books).

Schon, D. (1987) *Educating the reflective practitioner: Towards a new design for teaching and learning in the professions* (San Francisco: Jossey-Bass).

Schreiber, P. and Frank, E. (1983) 'The use of peer supervision by social work clinicians', *Clinical Supervisors*. 1(1), 29–36.

SCIE (2004) *Learning organisations: A self assessment resource pack* (London: Social Care Institute for Excellence).

Scottish Government (2006) *Changing lives: Report of the 21st century social work review* (Edinburgh: Scottish Government).

Scottish Government (2007) *Criminal Justice Directorate Circular 15/2006*. [online] http://www.scotland.gov.uk/Publications/2007/10/03110820/0 (Accessed 13 October 2013).

Scottish Government (2012) R*eshaping care for older people (*Edinburgh: Scottish Government).

Senge, P. M. (1990) *The fifth discipline: The art and practice of the learning organization* (New York: Doubleday).

Shaw, R. (2013) 'A model of the transformative journey into reflexivity: An exploration into students' experiences of critical reflection', *Reflective Practice: International and multidisciplinary perspectives*, 14, 319–335.

Smith, M. (2000) 'Supervision of fear in social work: a re-evaluation of reassurance', *Journal of Social Work Practice*, 14, 17–26.

Social Work (Scotland) Act (1968) http://www.legislation.gov.uk/ukpga/1968/49/contents (Accessed 13 October 2013).

SSSC. (2004). *Codes of practice for social service workers and employers*. http://www.sssc.uk.com/doc_details/1020-sssc-codes-of-practice-for-social-service-workers-and-employers (Accessed 13 October 2013).

Stamm, B. H. (2002) 'Measuring compassion satisfaction as well as fatigue: Developmental history of the compassion satisfaction and fatigue test', in C.R. Figley, (ed.), *Treating compassion fatigue* (New York: Brunner-Routledge), 107–119.

Stanford, S. (2010) '"Speaking back' to fear: Responding to the moral dilemmas of risk in social work practice,' *British Journal of Social Work*, 40, 1065–1080.

Stanton, N. (2004) *Mastering communication* (Basingstoke: Palgrave Macmillan).

Sudberry, J. (2002) 'Key features of therapeutic practice: the use of relationship', *Journal of Social Work Practice*, 16, 149–162.

Sutton, C. (1979) *Psychology for social workers and counsellors* (London: Routledge and Kegan Paul).

Tallant, C., Sambrook, M. and Green, S. (2008) 'Enagagement skills: best practice or effective practice?', in S. Green, E. Lancaster and S. Feasey (eds.), *Addressing offending behaviour: Context, practice and values* (Devon: Willan).

Taylor, B. (2010) *Reflective Practice for Healthcare Professionals*, 3rd edition (Maidenhead: McGraw-Hill Education).

Taylor, C. and White, S. (2006) 'Knowledge and reasoning in social work: Educating for humane judgement', *British Journal of Social Work*, 36, 937–954.

Taylor, M. (2007) 'Professional dissonance: A promising concept for clinical social work'. *Smith College Studies in Social Work* 77, 89–99.

Thomas, J. and Spreadbury, K. (2008) 'Promoting best practice through supervision, support and communities of practice', in K. Jones, B. Cooper and H. Ferguson (eds.), *Best practice in social work: Critical perspectives* (Basingstoke: Palgrave Macmillan), 251–256.

Thompson, N. (2009) *People skills*, 3rd edition (Basingstoke: Palgrave Macmillan).

Thompson, S. and Thompson, N. (2008) *The critically reflective practitioner* (Basingstoke: Palgrave Macmillan).

Thornton, D. (2007) *Scoring guide for Risk Matrix 2000.9/SVC* http://www.bhamlive1.bham.ac.uk/Documents/college-les/psych/RM2000scoringinstructions.pdf (Accessed 13 October 2013).

Thorsen, C.A., and DeVore, S. (2012) 'Analysing reflection on/for action: A new approach', *Reflective Practice: International and multidisciplinary perspectives*, 14(1), 88–103.

Trevithick, P. (2005) *Social work skills*, 2nd edition (Maidenhead: Open University Press).

Trotter, C. (2006) *Working with involuntary clients: A guide to practice*, 2nd edition (London: Sage).

Turner, J. and Stets, J. (2005) *The sociology of emotions* (Cambridge University Press).

Van Lanen, M.T.A. (2008) 'Peeping at peers: a cross-national study of professionalism in social work', *European Journal of Social Work*, 11(4), 469–473.

Ward, A. (2010) 'The learning relationship: Learning and development for relationship-based practice', in G. Ruch, D. Turney, and A. Ward (eds.) *Relationship-based social work: Getting to the heart of practice* (London: Jessica Kingsley), 183–199.

Webb, S. (2006) *Social work in a risk society: Social and political perspectives* (Basingstoke: Palgrave Macmillan).

Webb, S. A. (2007) 'The comfort of strangers: Social work, modernity and late-Victorian England – part 1', *European Journal of Social Work*, 10, 39–54.

White, S., Fook, J. and Gardner, F. (2006) (eds.) *Critical reflection in health and social care* (Maidenhead: McGraw-Hill).

Whittaker, A. (2011) 'Social defences and organisational culture in a local authority child protection setting: challenges for the Munro review?', *Journal of Social Work Practice: Psychotherapeutic approaches in the health, welfare and the community*, 25(4), 481–495.

Wilson, K., Ruch, G., Lymbery, M. and Cooper, A. (2011) Social work: *An introduction to contemporary practice*, 2nd edition (London: Pearson Education).

Yip, K. (2006) 'Self reflection in reflective practice: a note for caution', *British Journal of Social Work*, 36, 777–788.

Index

actuarial fallacy, 88
anti-oppressive practice, 3, 16, 19,
    59, 60, 68, 79, 80, 82
assessment,
    in case notes, 121, 128
    and critical reflection, 63, 66
    and emotions, 45, 58–60
    influencing factors, 40, 53–57
    and intervention, 63, 71–74
    and listening, 79
    and power, empowerment, 60–63
    pre-birth, 79, 82
    process of, 52, 63–65
    re-assessment, 19
    reflective assessment, 53
    reflection, role of, 57, 58
    reports, 65
    risk assessment, 88, 90, 92,
        97–100
    standardized assessment tools,
        55–57, 97
    and value base, 60–63
    time pressures, 53
authoritative role of social
    workers, 45

care management, 70
care plans
    and assessment, 61
    and records/writing, 119
case notes
    assessment in, 121, 128
    and reflection/critical reflection,
        24–26, 126, 128, 142, 144,
        157
    and writing/records, 119, 120,
        144

accuracy, 125
    and decision making, 128, 148
child protection
    and life changing assessments,
        57, 60
    and authoritative role of social
        workers, 45
    case conference, 108
    child-centred, 4
    empowerment issues, 60, 108,
        113
    evolution of, 73
    and intervention/intervening
        organization, 74, 151
    pre-birth/unborn child
        protection, 61, 79
    and risk assessment/decisions,
        88
    lack of social workers'
        autonomy/managerialism/
        bureaucracy, 10, 54, 55, 61
    plans/records, 88
    uncertainty in, 89, 151
codes of ethics, 5, 8
codes of practice, 5, 6, 8, 122, 125
communication, 9, 10, 20, 31,
    35–49, 74, 97, 120, 127, 144,
    148, 153, 157
criminal justice social work, 86, 91
critical reflection
    and assessment, 63, 66
    and awareness of power/power
        dynamics, 109
    and case notes/ reports/written
        record keeping/diary, 15, 27
    and communication/interaction,
        38, 39, 43

critical reflection (*cont.*)
definition of, 13, 17
and disjuncture, 12, 13
and emotions, 10, 11, 31, 38,
40, 46, 146, 150
framework of, 23
and hard features of social
work, 33, 149
key aspects of, 20
and organizations, 140, 145,
146, 151–154
and Professional Capabilities
Framework (PCF), 1, 5, 7,
150
questions for, 30, 31
and reflexivity, 29
and risk decisions, 85, 93, 97,
98, 100
role in ethical practice, 115
and social work/social workers,
8, 19, 32, 55, 130
and supervision, 99, 137–139
and support, 141
and values, 13, 63, 146, 150
and writing/recording/case notes,
117, 119, 120, 122,
126–128, 144

defensible decisions and
judgements, 63, 88, 89, 90,
93
risk decisions, 85, 88
defensive (ness), 90, 100,
111–114, 154
desistance, 92–95, 149
disjuncture, 12, 13, 47, 48, 60, 61,
78, 95, 96, 98, 111, 115, 134,
141
double-loop
learning, 17, 19, 150
reflection, 20, 66
thinking, 81, 83

emotional intelligence, 9, 11, 20,
31, 54, 58, 62, 79, 92, 136

emotions (also emotional)
and assessment, 50, 58, 60, 62,
63, 66
and codes of practice, 6, 7, 139
and communication/interaction,
37, 38, 40, 42
and critically informed
interventions, 71, 72, 75,
77, 78, 92
definition of/meaning of, 11, 12,
41
and ethics, 78
and meetings, 91, 105, 113
and reflection/critical reflection,
1, 5, 9–11, 13, 14, 20, 23,
24, 30–31, 38, 40, 46, 79,
99, 121, 123, 146, 150
and reflective social work
practitioner model, 14
and reflective social work
organization model, 156
and relationships, 48, 83, 100,
113
and soft features of social work,
2, 3, 6, 21, 22, 75, 124,
149
and supervision, 33, 78, 99, 146
and writing/recording/case notes,
121, 123–126
of service users, 57–59, 61, 66,
80
role of organizations/
organizational culture, 43,
114, 155, 156
of/impact on social work/er, 3–5,
9, 10, 32, 33, 37, 44–47,
59, 60, 63, 66, 69, 77, 78,
80, 132, 133, 135, 148
empowerment
awareness, 148
assessment and, 50, 52, 60, 64
in child protection, 60, 108, 113
intervention, 84
in organisations, 145
and power, 39, 43, 109

and service user, 60, 64, 84,
110, 114
ethics, 5–8, 47, 76, 78, 79, 115, 150
codes of ethics, 8

group dynamics, 101, 105, 106
groupthink, 106–108, 110, 111,
115

hard features of social work, 2, 3,
13, 21, 33, 42, 60, 65, 75, 76,
81, 83, 148, 149, 151
human rights, 7, 59, 63, 95–98

intervention, 14–16, 62, 63,
68–84, 89, 96, 148, 157

learning culture, 123, 143
legislation, 48, 59, 65, 75, 79, 81,
100, 125, 126, 145, 146, 148,
149

managerialism, 2, 13, 55, 89
MAPPA, 36, 85, 87, 90–94, 96
meetings
and code of ethics, 115
decision making, 103, 104, 112,
148
and emotions/emotional
intelligence, 32, 92,
112–114, 150
and participation/contribution,
109, 110, 113, 115, 116,
153
and policy, 104
power dynamics, 41, 42, 91, 92,
104, 105, 107, 109, 110,
113, 115
reflective dialogue, 27
and reflection, 39, 90, 93,
104–106, 109, 111, 113,
115
and reflexivity, 108, 109
skills/approach, 39, 92, 105
and strategies, 111, 112

methods of reflection, 17, 24
models of reflection, 17, 21, 22,
24, 34, 66

non-verbal communication, 42

offenders, 45, 86, 88, 90–92, 94,
130, 132
organizational culture, 3, 5, 21,
37, 41–43, 55, 124, 130, 133,
141, 146, 152–155

paperwork, 56, 65, 72, 119
see also care plans, case notes,
record keeping, reports
peer support, 26, 27, 54, 130, 134
policy
and/application to, practice, 1,
2, 5
and case notes/writing, 120, 125
and communication, 41
and hard features of social
work, 2, 13, 21, 60, 65, 75,
81, 83, 146, 149
and impact on practice/people/
decision making, 56, 60, 92
key initiatives, 4, 5
and meetings, 104
national, 73, 138, 150
organizational, 71, 77
and reflective social work
practitioner model, 14, 48,
100, 146
and reflective social work
organization model, 156
and relationships, 5, 95
role in assessment, 56, 60, 73
role in intervention, 71, 73, 75,
77, 84, 95
and soft features of social work,
6, 8, 13, 95, 149, 150
power
assessment and 50, 52, 60, 63
awareness of, 18, 20, 29, 31,
39, 109, 110

power *(cont.)*
  and codes of practice, 6, 39
  dynamics of, 9, 16, 19, 20, 21,
    29, 42, 43, 60, 63, 101,
    104, 108, 109, 110, 115,
    116, 130, 148
  meetings and, 104, 106, 108,
    110, 113, 115, 116, 148
  reflection on, 71
  statutory, 18, 79
power dynamics
  awareness of, 110
  challenge, 19, 20, 66, 81, 149
  critical reflection of, 109
  meetings, 104, 108, 110, 111,
    116, 148
  supervision, 134
  understanding of, 20, 111
powerlessness, 109
professionalism, 30, 33, 124–126,
  150–152

questioning, 23, 24, 30, 39, 59,
  77

rational–technical approach, 2, 3,
  5, 17, 20, 21, 81
record keeping, (Chapter 8), 4, 18,
  19, 24–27, 30, 34, 54, 56, 57,
  58, 64, 99, 142, 148, 157
  see also care plans, case notes,
    reports
reflective social work organisation
  model, 156
reflective social work practitioner
  model, 13, 14, 30, 33, 66,
  127, 155
reflective writing, 25, 27, 30,
  122–124
reflective dialogue, 26, 27, 153
reflexivity
  and critical reflection, 20, 29
  and soft features of social work,
    33
  and supervision, 63

aspects of, 17
meaning/definitions of, 29, 33,
  77, 104
questions for, 30, 31
use/role of (in meetings/
  interactions), 33, 47, 59,
  77, 97, 104, 106, 109, 113,
  115, 148
and emotions, 121
and writing/records/case notes,
  128
and supervision, 143
and double-loop learning, 150
and reflective organizations, 153
relationship based social work,
  8–10, 43, 49, 95, 113, 125,
  126, 133, 141, 152
reports, 56, 119–121, 125, 126,
  128
resistance, 35, 43–47, 95
risk assessment, 50, 85, 88, 90,
  92, 97
risk aversion, 3, 12, 85, 89, 90,
  93–95, 99, 100
risk decisions, 85, 88–90, 95, 96, 98
risk management, 93, 133

single-loop learning/practice/
  reflection, 17, 18, 44, 66, 81,
  82
social justice, 7, 13, 56, 59, 80
soft features of social work, 2, 5,
  7, 8, 13, 17, 33, 38, 68, 71,
  75, 78, 81, 146–150, 158
status, 10, 79, 91, 105, 107, 108,
  111–113, 116, 120, 122
supervision, (Chapter 9), 5, 9, 10,
  16, 25–27, 33, 51, 54, 55, 59,
  63, 68, 78, 84, 85, 99, 102,
  117, 121, 123, 148, 151,
  154–157
SuReCom model for supervision,
  153, 155

uncertainty, 29, 89, 90, 151, 157

values
  challenges to, 12, 125
  codes of practice and ethics, 6,
    7, 12
  and communication, 37, 41, 42,
    47, 48
  and complexities, 3, 4, 66, 80,
    91, 92, 93
  and decision making, 58, 59, 98,
    126, 148
  and disjuncture, 12, 13, 60, 61,
    62, 63, 71, 78, 95, 96, 100,
    115
  and emotions, 82, 99, 119, 123,
    146
  and interaction, 5, 10
  and interventions, 74
  and reflexivity, 29–31, 111, 115,
    150, 158
  and risk aversion, 95, 100
  and soft features, 21, 75, 124,
    125, 149, 151
  and supervision, 134
  and professionalism, 150, 151
  Professional Capabilities,
    Framework (PCF), 5, 7
  and soft features of social work,
    2, 3
value base, 4, 7, 9

written recording: see care plans,
  case notes, record keeping,
  reports